PRAISE

for *The Advisor Transformation*
and Shawn Sparks

"From success to significance–this transformative read is essential for financial advisors driven by purpose and aiming to make a massive impact."

—Tim Tebow

"This isn't just another book for financial advisors; it's a roadmap for those who truly desire to redefine their practice, elevate the impact they make, and enrich the lives of all those they serve. Any advisor aiming to build a comprehensive business—one that thrives for themselves, energizes their team, and delivers unparalleled value to clients—will find this book not just useful, but indispensable. An unmissable read in today's complex financial landscape."

—Daniel Crosby, Ph.D., author of *The Laws of Wealth*

"If you truly aspire to build your business to scale, don't just read this book—devour it. But when you are done, don't keep it a secret. Hand this to your team so that you can all be on the same page and aligned on how to build your business to significance."

—Derek Gregoire, cofounder SHP Financial

"In Brazilian Jiu-Jitsu, we learn that with the right techniques, even a smaller person can handle larger opponents effectively. *The Advisor Transformation* mirrors this principle, offering advisors the techniques to achieve more with less time and effort. If you are a financial advisor who wants to succeed in business and life, this is a must read."

—Rener Gracie, WSJ best selling author,
Brazilian jiu-jitsu master and entrepreneur

"The world doesn't just need more financial advisors—it needs financial leaders. *The Advisor Transformation* is a calling for those ready to step up and guide clients with insights, passion, and integrity. If you aim to be the preeminent financial leader in your market, this book is an unequivocal must-read. Dive in and be transformed."

—**Chris Smith,** The Campfire Effect™

"In today's fiercely competitive financial advisory arena, growth and scale demand more than just strong marketing and sales. You must grasp the crucial elements that are not merely beneficial but indispensable. *The Advisor Transformation* illuminates these essentials. For those determined to soar to unprecedented heights, this book is your roadmap."

—**Anthony Pellegrino**, founder, Goldstone Financial

"Transform your advisory practice from just another job to a business you truly love. *The Advisor Transformation* is your blueprint to achieving wealth, freedom, and a lifestyle that aligns with your dreams. Don't just work; thrive in a venture you're passionate about."

—**Justin Donald**, number-one *WSJ* and *USA Today* best-selling author, founder of The Lifestyle Investor, host of *The Lifestyle Investor* Podcast

"Some books are strategic, others tactical…a rare few are both. *The Advisor Transformation* is one of them! This book takes the complexities of financial services and decodes them through proven frameworks, allowing the reader to build a better business, without sacrificing all that REALLY matters in the process. The clever use of visual frameworks and models acts as 'blueprints for the brain' that allow the reader to see the transition from idea to action. This leads to a more predictable speed of execution. I'm privileged to have witnessed advisors who are already applying the ideas shared, to enjoying the growth, freedom, and joy promised. This is available to anyone who reads and applies the lessons shared within these pages."

—**Simon Bowen**, founder The Models Method, Creator The Genius Mode

"*The Advisor Transformation* is a profound exploration of what it truly means to be a top-tier advisor in today's complex world. If you aspire to achieve greater success and leave a significant legacy, then this book is for you!"

—**Ian Morgan Cron**, author of *The Road Back to You*

"*The Advisor Transformation* is like having a heart-to-heart chat on achieving success without the burnout. It's the guidebook on how to scale big without losing your spark or missing out on life's best moments. If you want to grow a business that makes an impact and still enjoy your life, this book is your roadmap."

—**Amy Porterfield**, author of New York Times Bestseller *Two Weeks Notice*

"*The Advisor Transformation* is a true gift for any financial advisor aiming to build a business of significance. Much like thoughtful gifting creates lasting bonds and opens doors to amazing opportunities, this book provides the essential tools and insights for advisors to deepen their client relationships, stand out in a crowded industry, and cultivate a business that's not just successful, but truly meaningful. Every page is a step toward transformation, making this book a must-have for those ready to elevate their impact and leave a legacy that matters."

—**John Ruhlin**, best-selling author and founder of GIFT•OLOGY

"In the relentless pursuit of success, it's all too easy to lose sight of what truly matters—our families. *The Advisor Transformation* isn't just a guide for elevating your business; it's a lifeline for reclaiming balance in your life. We have devoted our lives to helping families make the most of their precious time together, and we believe this book is a crucial tool for any advisor looking to do the same."

—**Jim and Jamie Sheils** , WSJ best-selling authors

"*The Advisor Transformation* is a revolutionary resource, perfectly aligned with the ethos we've built at Nitrogen. Just as we empower wealth management firms to navigate the journey from prospect to loyal client with precision and confidence, this book provides financial advisors with the tools they need to transform their practice from success to significance."

—**Aaron Klein**, co-founder and CEO at Nitrogen

"Books have the extraordinary power to transform lives and *The Advisor Transformation* is a testament to that belief. With proven strategies and actionable insights, *The Advisor Transformation* is your guide to thriving in both business and life. It's time to take control, elevate your practice, and create a lasting impact. Dive in, harness the power within these pages, and watch as your advisory practice transforms before your eyes."

—**Chandler Bolt**, CEO of selfpublishing.com, Forbes 30 Under 30 honoree, and seven-time bestselling author

"Is it possible to take your business to the next level without losing yourself in the process? Only if you follow the map offered in *The Advisor Transformation*! With specific sections focused on leveraging your team, your technology, and your capital, Shawn Sparks gives you everything you need to ignite your growth and scale your enterprise. As the famous adage notes, 'if you want to go far, go together.' With this book as your guide, there is no limit as to the heights you can reach!"

—**Joey Coleman**, keynote speaker and Wall Street Journal best selling author of *Never Lose a Customer Again*

"I wish I had *The Advisor Transformation* when I first started running my advisory firm. Shawn offers advisors a step-by-step framework of how to truly scale and maximize the impact they can make."

—**Dave Zoller**, CFP Streamline My Practice

"*The Advisor Transformation* is not just a book—it's a wake-up call. In a world where grinding it out just leads to physical exhaustion, this guide is your roadmap to a whole new way of dominating business and life. I've incorporated these lessons into my business, and it's changed my life. I highly recommend you do the same, but be careful as you may unlock a whole new way of thinking and the ability to build a future more exciting than you ever could have imagined."

—**Tom Jacobs**, founder of Jacobs Financial

"Obtaining unparalleled personal freedom while simultaneously propelling business growth can feel like an elusive goal, but this book brings it into reach. Shawn not only imparts tactical wisdom but unveils a comprehensive blueprint for scaling a financial advice business without burning out. A must-read for every advisor."

—**Robert Sofia**, chairman and CEO of Snappy Kraken

DOWNLOAD THE AUDIOBOOK FREE!

AS A THANK YOU FOR BUYING MY BOOK, I WOULD LIKE TO GIVE YOU THE AUDIOBOOK FOR FREE

Read it in the car, on a walk, or in your spare time and unlock the exciting future that this book can help you create.

Your transformation awaits; get the audiobook for FREE at the link below.

THEADVISORTRANSFORMATION.COM

THE ADVISOR TRANSFORMATION

TRIAD
PARTNERS

Published by Triad Partners, LLC

THE ADVISOR TRANSFORMATION

THE ULTIMATE GUIDE TO GROWTH, FREEDOM, AND JOY FOR FINANCIAL ADVISORS

SHAWN SPARKS

This publication is designed to provide general information regarding the subject matter covered. However, laws and practices often vary from state to state and are subject to change. Be sure to review and understand the laws and regulations in each state in which you conduct business.

This book has been written to assist financial advisors (herein referred to as "advisors") who are properly registered with a fee-based Registered Investment Advisory firm. Individuals who are not registered as such may not offer financial planning or advisory services, or provide specific advice to consumers on investments and/or financial plans.

This book includes a number of suggestions for ways that advisors can provide clients and prospects with certain benefits such as nominal gifts, meals, or forms of entertainment. Keep in mind that state insurance departments often have regulations that outline what types of gifts (including dollar amount thresholds) insurance professionals can give to consumers. In addition, your broker/dealer or Registered Investment Advisor may also have gifting limits for consumers that you should be familiar with. To protect your practice, be sure to understand and follow all rebating and gifting laws in the states in which you conduct business.

The author and publisher have taken reasonable precautions in the preparation of this book and believe the facts presented within are accurate as of the date it was written. However, neither the author nor the publisher assumes any responsibility for any errors or omissions. The author and publisher specifically disclaim any liability resulting from the use or application of the information contained in this book, and the information is not intended to serve as legal, financial, or other professional advice related to individual situations.

ISBN: 978-1-962894-01-2

Published by Triad Partners, LLC. For ordering information or special discounts for bulk purchases, please contact:

Shawn Sparks
730 New Hampshire St #222
Lawrence, KS 66044
(785) 830-0000
www.theadvisortransformation.com

DEDICATION

To the financial advisors I have had the privilege of working with over the years, it is with deep gratitude that I dedicate this book to you. From the moment that I entered this business, I fell in love with you as people, much more than the business itself. I saw your passion for helping your clients and your unwavering commitment to your mission. You taught me so much about the financial industry and allowed me to join you on your journey.

However, I also saw firsthand the challenges you faced—the endless meetings, the weight of responsibility, and the exhaustion that came with success. I knew you wanted something more, something better—a way to build your business that aligned with your vision and brought your dreams to life.

That's why I made it my life's work to help you transform in a better way. I turned my professional career upside down and started over, pouring my time, focus, energy, and resources into creating a proven framework in order to make your dreams a reality.

This book is the culmination of that work and my commitment to you. It is a roadmap to help you build your business to significance and scale. I am fully committed to supporting you every step of the way.

Thank you for inspiring me, for trusting me, and for allowing me to be part of your journey. It is an honor to dedicate this book to you and to help your dreams come true.

ACKNOWLEDGMENTS

One of the greatest blessings in life is to wake up every day excited about what you do. Much of that depends on who you spend your time working with. I have been fortunate to have worked with many incredible advisors over the last seventeen years. I have witnessed firsthand how a financial advisor's business can evolve over time, from zero to scale.

Many people view their business associates with one lens and their friends with another. I've never considered the advisors I work with simply advisors, clients, or business associates. I've always viewed them as friends. I know without a doubt that they've viewed me in the same way, which has made my experiences in this business much more meaningful and joyful. *The Advisor Transformation* was made possible because these advisors gave me the blessing of taking part in their businesses and listening to the conversations in their own heads—the ones driving their businesses and their future dreams. They have trusted me to help them, and I have not taken that lightly.

While I can't possibly thank everyone by name who has helped me, I'd like to thank some who highly influenced *The Advisor Transformation*. First, I want to thank my wonderful wife, Aubrey. There are certain times in life when true love and loyalty are tested, and I haven't always been sure how Aubrey would react to my crazy ideas. Yet she has not only supported me but also encouraged me to pursue my dreams in life and in business. I would not be where I am—or who I am—without Aubrey.

I'd also like to thank our four wonderful kids—Sadie, AnnMarie, Sutton, and Charlotte. Seeing these four beautiful people each day and seeing what's most important to them has enabled me to make better decisions and create the right vision for our family's future. They're helping me create not mere success but meaningful success and significance. Coming home and having them run to me with a smile always changes my world for the better, regardless of the struggles, challenges, or pitfalls I've experienced that day.

Thank you to my wonderful team at Triad Partners. No dream comes alive without a wonderful team to push it forward. Having you all join me and believe in this mission is one of the greatest blessings I've received. #LetsGrow **#DBDL**

I have struggled with how to thank and acknowledge the many advisors who collectively contributed to this book. They number in the thousands, yet each of them is the perfect example of what it takes to scale and build a business that rewards everyone with more growth, freedom, and joy. Many people reach success, but very few are equipped with the foundational knowledge that enables others to join in that success or create it for themselves. Thanks for the amazing lessons you've taught me, our team, and our advisors and for helping blaze a trail that others can follow.

Even though I cannot list you each by name, I am aware that I owe you all a debt of gratitude for the life and business lessons you've taught me over the years.[1] Please know that you have a friend in me who's always willing to help you whenever I can. I hope this book serves as a small token of my appreciation and helps you in your own quest for a business and life.

1 To protect the privacy of my advisors, I have withheld their names. Many of the stories in this book come from individual advisors with whom I have worked. However, some of the stories combine the experiences of several advisors into a single story to clarify and strengthen a point.

CONTENTS

Foreword

FOREWORD

Success.

What does it mean?

In the fast-paced world of financial services, success often means lucrative financial rewards and accomplishments at the expense of the advisor's personal health and family. Worse, all too often the more successful financial advisors become, the less freedom and joy they experience.

This naturally leads to this question: if your business doesn't lead to a better overall life, is what you have success at all?

In *The Advisor Transformation,* Shawn Sparks, a long-time business coach to financial advisors and author of *The Advisor Breakthrough*, shares how financial advisors can build a business of significance, one that enhances both their professional and their personal life.

Through emotionally charged, personal examples of the hardships that he's witnessed as financial advisors have climbed the deceptive "ladder of success," Shawn shares how building a business model to scale can lead to more for everyone in this industry. More happiness. More freedom, more impact, more growth, and more purpose.

The Advisor Transformation challenges everyone in the financial services industry to think differently. What if you can build a business that was less dependent on you for it to grow? What if the more successful your business becomes, the more your team enjoys their jobs? What if you can grow your business without sacrificing your life?

Drawing upon years of industry experience, Shawn debunks what we've been conditioned to believe about success—that it requires extreme sacrifice that ultimately leads to burnout. Instead, this step-by-step guide shows a new path to success, one that leads to a thriving business and an incredible quality of life.

The true essence of this book lies in this timely reminder: businesses should be built as if our very lives depend on them–because they do. It's not just about putting up big numbers. It's about building a business that makes a massive difference for all of those who touch it. One where success aligns with constant growth and inspiration, along with freedom and joy.

Whether you're just getting started on this journey or are a seasoned professional teetering on the edge of burnout, *The Advisor Transformation* is for you. It offers invaluable insights to help you build your business in an entirely different way that will redefine success, rekindle your passion, and help you reclaim a business and life that you truly deserve.

Embrace this guide and let it steer you toward a horizon where business success and personal fulfillment coexist. After all, isn't that the ultimate goal?

As someone who has worked across countless business sectors, I have witnessed—firsthand—countless business owners who reach for what we traditionally view as success—money, notoriety—only to realize that they've sacrificed the very essence of the life that they truly cherish most to get there: their family, their time, their joy, and their health.

The profound truths about success, significance, and scale shared in *The Advisor Transformation* are valuable not just in the financial world, but in all industries. This isn't just about how advisors can transform their business. It's about how all business owners can change their mindset to start living and loving their business and life.

—Michael Hyatt

SECTION 1

PURPOSE

More than 70 percent of rookie financial advisors fail[2]. Those who persevere find success, and a select few achieve an extraordinary level of it. But this success often becomes a double-edged sword, leading to a plateau in growth and an overwhelming sense of burnout. Their business, which once promised freedom and prosperity, becomes a chain that binds them.

Ask yourself: If your business success doesn't enhance your quality of life, is it truly success?

I firmly believe it's not. If you're feeling trapped in the very success you've built, you've structured your business the wrong way. Life is too fleeting, too precious to be spent building a business that doesn't uplift your existence. The tragedy isn't just in chasing success; it's in achieving it and then realizing it's not what you truly wanted.

But what if there's another way?

What if there's a way where you can build an extraordinary business that blesses your life as opposed to one that becomes your life—a way that doesn't force you to choose between professional success and personal fulfillment.

This is where the **Do Business Do Life (#DBDL)** approach comes in. It's not about the traditional sense of work/life balance; it's about work/life integration. It's about intertwining your professional aspirations with your personal dreams, letting one enhance the other.

Work is a big part of your overall life. Why wouldn't you grow and improve work and your life at the same time? Then, the more successful your business is, the better quality of life you'll have as

2 https://www.barrons.com/advisor/articles/financial-advisor-talent-shortage-cerulli-69010ca9#:~:text=Although%2018%2C207%20new%20trainees%20entered,2%2C459%20advisors%20retired%20in%202022.

well. This is the true prize and the outcome of your work. Every advisor deserves to build a business that gives them unlimited growth, freedom, and joy.

Every advisor deserves to build a business that gives them unlimited growth, freedom, and joy.

I've dedicated my life to guiding advisors toward that vision. But here's the catch: I can light the path, provide the tools, and share the wisdom, but the journey? That's on you. The desire, the drive, the commitment—it has to come from within.

I collaborate with advisors who resonate with this vision, who yearn for the **#DBDL** life. And together, we make it a reality.

The first section of *The Advisor Transformation* is about purpose. Why are you here? What do you want to be remembered for? Why do you want a business that scales? How are you going to get it? What do you want to accomplish in your business, and what impact do you ultimately want your business to have on those who are in your life? Are you committed enough to these wants that you'll finish this book? Most people don't finish the books they start. Be the exception. Read *The Advisor Transformation* all the way through, and learn how to truly transform your business and your life.

Very few people reach a point in life where they can truly say they understand their purpose. Most strive for money or status, but ultimately they end up somewhere they don't want to be. When you are authentic in your purpose, you will arrive at the proper destination.

This understanding is critical to scale. If you don't identify this as your motivation, you won't persevere through the many battles and decisions it takes to truly scale.

Are you ready to #DBDL?

1

THE PRICE OF SUCCESS: WHY YOU NEED A BUSINESS THAT SCALES

Dad, you're always on your phone for work. Can't it wait?

— A plea from the 11-year-old son of a top advisor

Anthony is a high-energy, achievement-focused individual. He's a hard worker who is always looking to grow and improve. He has succeeded at whatever he's put his mind to. He thinks in big ways and always sets big goals. He's smart, well-spoken, and one of the most trustworthy and likable people I know. That combination of skills and temperament makes him a perfect fit for the role of financial advisor. When he entered the industry, he felt like he'd found his true calling.

Anthony approached the financial services business with the same drive he brings to every endeavor. He had a clear focus on being the best and set out to learn everything he could to succeed. At industry events, he took advantage of down time to sit with more seasoned advisors and pepper them with questions. Eventually, they asked Anthony for a break so they could relax a little. Even so, they admired his determination. He was on a mission to build a successful business that would put his young family ahead financially, and nothing was going to stop him. He saw himself as one of the most hardworking, successful financial advisors in the country. And that's exactly what he became.

Anthony's business soared in record time. He reached financial goals that most advisors don't reach in their lifetime. As an individual advisor, he brought in well over $60 million in new assets per year. Before long, Anthony became the guy new advisors sought out for advice. At industry events, he was recognized as a top producer, often lauded for single handedly bringing in more new business than some teams of five or six advisors.

That made Anthony feel great about himself and his business. His hard work and dedication had paid off. He had set out to become one of the elite producers in the industry, and that's exactly what he achieved. His dream of success had come true.

Then one day when Anthony was home with his family, his young children asked him to come outside. He gladly joined them in the backyard to throw the football around. Just as his son tossed him the ball, Anthony's phone rang. It was a work call.

"Kids," he said, "I need a few minutes." But Anthony's young children were eager to spend time with their dad, so they pleaded with him.

"Come on, Dad! You said you'd play with us. You always do this!"

Meanwhile, Anthony was on the phone with a client, covering one ear with his hand, trying to conduct business. The kids tugged at his pant leg. "Would you believe this?" Anthony told me later. "I wound up in my bedroom closet—one hand holding the door shut, my head stuck between my suits to drown out my kids' voices—just so I could take a business call after hours."

Twenty minutes later, Anthony realized what had happened. He had lost time with his children, time he would never get back. That evening as he tucked his kids into bed, his son asked, "Dad, you're always on your phone for work. Can't it wait?"

Ouch!

As painful as that moment was and as guilty as Anthony felt, this wasn't the last straw for Anthony. That came a few months later at a large industry conference designed to kick off the beginning of the year. Thousands of advisors from all over the country attended to celebrate the top industry achievements from the previous year. Anthony was proud to be one of the top achievers. As Anthony walked across the stage, his industry peers gave him a rousing ovation. But later, Anthony told me that the thrill of being one of the top dogs in the industry wore off quickly. In fact, right after Anthony walked off the stage, he went straight to the bathroom, splashed water on his face, and looked himself in the eyes in the bathroom mirror.

"That's when it finally hit me," Anthony said. "All that work I'd done was for seven seconds of applause. And when the calendar turned over, I'd have to start all over again. That's when I knew the cost to my family was just too high. 'I can't do this anymore,' I told myself. 'I'm done.'"

Anthony realized that he had reached burnout.

Burnout is defined as "physical, emotional, or mental exhaustion, accompanied by decreased motivation, lowered performance, and negative attitudes toward oneself and others."—*APA Dictionary of Psychology*.

Signs of burnout:

- Physical exhaustion
- Lack of presence
- Feeling apathetic or dissatisfied with your work
- High stress and irritability
- Changes to diet or sleep patterns

Anthony was tired and frustrated with both his job and his life. He was also losing sleep over working more than he could handle. He wasn't spending enough time with his family, and he no longer enjoyed a business he used to love. Was he depressed? Stressed? Just overwhelmed? Regardless, he had realized his business was not enhancing the overall quality of his life. It was trying to consume his life.

Anthony was also distraught that in his determination to become the best in his field, he had sacrificed something of even greater value—his family. The money and recognition meant nothing because he didn't have adequate time to enjoy the fruit of that labor with his family. Anthony's career goal had conflicted with two other goals he'd never articulated—being a loving husband and being a present parent. He realized that the more successful he became at work, the more that success demanded from him and his family. In his role as an advisor, the process was simple math. More time and effort equal more business and more money. The only way to be more successful was to put in more time and effort and increase production. But in his role as a parent and spouse, this was the simple math: more quality time equals more joy and fulfillment. How could he do both?

Anthony quickly assumed that there were two ways to change his situation. He could:

1. Grow by brute force and continue sacrificing his family, free time, and happiness.
2. Grow as a person, spouse, and a dad and scale back his business by running what is known in this industry as a "lifestyle business."

However, Anthony didn't see how he could do either one and feel any better. He already felt enormous guilt about not spending time with his family, but he also knew he'd regret not growing his business.

Anthony couldn't see a third way or an option to do both. There was no option to do business and do life. So Anthony made the difficult choice to scale back his ambition in order to get his life back.

The consequences of option one were obvious to Anthony—

bad health, unhappiness, losing touch with the people he loved deeply. He had gone down this path for some time, and he realized the lies he had told himself along the way, including:

"I'm not doing this for me; I'm doing this for them."
"Just a little more, then I can get my life back."
"Once we get to this level of success, then I'll start living right."

Anthony knew he couldn't stay on that path. But option two? The consequences that come with that are not always immediately obvious. Yes, you lose some financial gain, but when an ambitious person like Anthony gives up growth, it often kills any joy they used to find in the business. Tony Robbins says growth is a basic human need, and when we give up progression, it steals the fun of the business entirely. Entrepreneurs love to grow their businesses—it's what gets them up each day, excited to go to work. Take that growth away, and I'll show you a very miserable person. A big part of the joy and fun of owning your own business is the pursuit of growth and progression. Right?

Choosing option two was the only option left for Anthony in that moment, but it would eventually cause him to fall out of love with the business. When entrepreneurs give up on their dreams and convert their businesses to a job, it's a sad situation for many of them.

Anthony knew the source of joy for him in this business was the ability to wake up each day excited to build an exciting future, a better tomorrow.

So both outcomes were really unfortunate and symbolic of throwing in the towel. Unfortunately, a lot of successful entrepreneurs end up facing this dilemma as they reach success with no other way to turn.

I've met hundreds of financial advisors just like Anthony and I can tell you that there is another way. You can learn to scale your business so there is no limit to your growth over time. You can do that and have more freedom as your business becomes more successful, all the while maintaining the joy that keeps you excited about your business. Anthony found another way. So have many others. Ultimately, you need to build a business that scales beyond you.

2

HOW *THE ADVISOR TRANSFORMATION* WORKS

According to a Fundera study,[3] 81 percent of business owners work overtime, and 89 percent work weekends. If this is you, you are in good company. But rest assured, there is a way to transform out of this, and it doesn't take as long as you think.

So how long does it take?

The answer? It depends on how badly you really want it.

3 https://www.fundera.com/blog/study-finds-business-owners-earn-less

Do you ever feel like you never have enough time in the day and that you are always working from behind?

Do you feel stuck in survival mode with no hope of getting out?

Do you feel pressure, anxiety, and constant worry that the business will fall apart if you aren't there?

Do you ever feel guilt or regret that you are giving too much to your business and not enough to your family and loved ones?

How badly do you want to build a real business that you own rather than one that owns you?

Don't just skim by those questions. Think about them for a minute, and then answer them honestly.

If you're early in your career and on the road to success, you might not yet feel the toll of burnout. You might even be thinking, "That won't happen to me." It's easy to feel that way when you're growing. Most advisors pursue success without the proper infrastructure, making the burnout outcome we've described inevitable. You do have the luxury of learning from the mistakes of others so you can avoid the pain they've felt. So pay close attention, regardless of where you are on your journey because I can help you make that transformation by sharing everything I know about advisors who have found a third way—one that will bring more growth, freedom, and joy to your life and business. But the willpower is yours.

The vision to help advisors get more growth, freedom, and joy in both their businesses and lives was created around the idea of building a business of significance. That means your business 100 percent supports the lifestyle you want to live. That is different than a lifestyle business (more on that later). It really comes down to Do Business, Do Life—**#DBDL**—a guiding philosophy that's designed to encourage individuals to integrate their personal and professional lives harmoniously. This concept transcends the conventional notion of balance and suggests that business and life are not separate entities but rather unified components that collaboratively enhance your overall quality of life. It offers a healthier, more fulfilling, and inspiring approach to living a well-rounded life.

This book, *The Advisor Transformation*, explains high-level concepts about how to scale your business so you can change your life. It's broken down into six sections that were intentionally developed to transform not just your marketing or sales efforts but also your entire business in order to improve your overall life.

The next section—Mindset—is the setup. It will get you to a place mentally where you have the belief that you need to have in yourself, your purpose, your team, and the possibility of change so you can approach this massive transformation. This is critical because so many advisors say yes to the idea of transformation, but when they hit the first roadblock, they give up and drift back to where they were before. Without a strong belief that this is what you want and that this is possible, you won't make it past that first roadblock, and transformation will not occur.

Only after you adjust your mindset can you change your life, which is why the five sections after Purpose and Mindset focus on Triad's Five Principles to Scale™. They include:

Triad's 5 Principles to Scale™

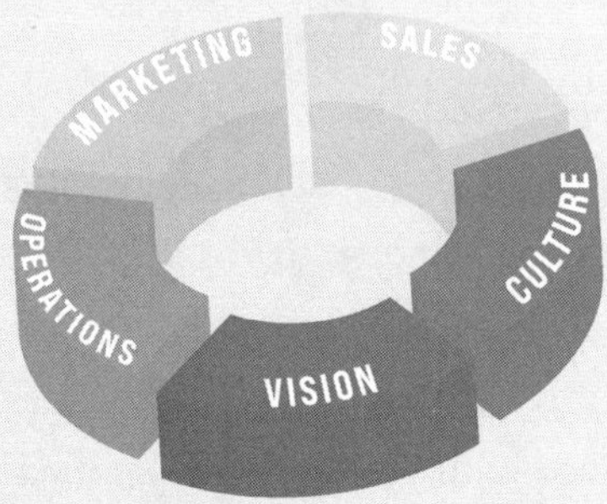

1. **Vision:** Where you're headed, clarity on how to get there, and an exciting plan for becoming who you want to be.
2. **Operations:** The infrastructure, foundations, and processes needed to optimize your performance and create raving fans.
3. **Marketing:** How you share what you do with your audience so that you can attract the right people for the right reason.
4. **Sales:** How to transfer the belief that you can help your ideal client to that client.
5. **Culture:** The environment that you create that gets people excited to show up to work and fulfill your mission.

None of these principles can function without the others. When one piece of the pie is missing, the rest starts to fall apart. They support and reinforce each other and are all necessary in order to create a business that gives you unlimited growth, freedom, and joy.

As you work your way through each of the next six sections, you will notice the following:

Transformational Targets: These open each chapter and outline top takeaways from that chapter.

Transformational Takeaways: These are found at the end of most chapters and are designed to give you a snapshot of the chapter's top lessons.

#DBDL icons: These highlight tidbits that help advisors #DBDL.

Enemies of Scale icons: These are the big mistakes many advisors make. We want you to recognize them and avoid them.

When you're finished with *The Advisor Transformation*, share it with your team. Not only are they helping you build your business, but the more they understand about business, the better your business will be.

Never in your life have you been closer to a transformation than you are right now. Let's get started!

SECTION 2

MINDSET

Remember what it was like on day one when you started your business? My guess is that you felt a lot like Anthony. You were super excited to get started—excited to find your first clients, excited to help them, and excited about both your professional and personal future. Right?

That was day one.

Amazon Founder Jeff Bezos has a theory about day one that is so powerful that he created Amazon's culture around it.[4]

Bezos said, "Day one is about being constantly curious, nimble, and experimental. It means being brave enough to fail if it means that by applying lessons learnt, we can better surprise and delight customers in the future."

Curious. Nimble. Experimental. Brave enough to fail. Is that what day one felt like for you? It's what day one of building Triad Partners, a business development company that only works with elite financial advisors, felt like to me. In fact, coming to work every day still feels like that.

> "Day 2 is stasis. Followed by irrelevance. Followed by excruciating, painful decline. Followed by death. And that is why it is always day 1."

4 https://aws.amazon.com/executive-insights/customers/sustaining-a-day-1-culture//

Bezos went on to add that organizations start to fail—move from entropy to mediocrity—when they hit day two. "Day 2 is stasis. Followed by irrelevance. Followed by excruciating, painful decline. Followed by death. And that is why it is always day 1."

To keep yourself (and your practice) in a day-one mentality, you have to constantly remain focused on the customer and your vision. You have to constantly be nimble, curious, experimental, and brave, and your team has to feel that from you too. If they don't, they will move to day two feelings in the blink of an eye.

So the first challenge as you work toward your transformation is to view each day like day one. It's to remain excited about where you're headed, nimble when serving your clients, and being brave enough to create the business and life you've always dreamed of. It's never too late to reinvent yourself and your business. No matter where your business is today, take the time you need to remember that day one feeling, and approach this transformational work with that day-one mindset. Throw away any excuses—or limitations—you've put on your dreams due to day-two thinking. Today is a new day. It is day one again. It's time to build the future you deserve.

The second challenge is to wholeheartedly believe in the possibility of your dreams. At Triad Partners, we often talk about the Trinity of Significance™, a triangle that shows the path to living a significant life—one where your business enhances the overall life you want to live—**#DBDL**.

First, you must believe that what you want to build is truly possible for you to attain. You have to believe that no matter what obstacles you face or who tells you it won't work, you believe in it 100 percent. No matter what happens, no matter who says no, you're convinced you will get this done. Forget your history. You have to believe wholeheartedly that this is your destiny from here on. You have to believe it is truly possible for you to be the exception. Without that belief, you will not take the action needed to get the results you want.

Trinity of Significance™

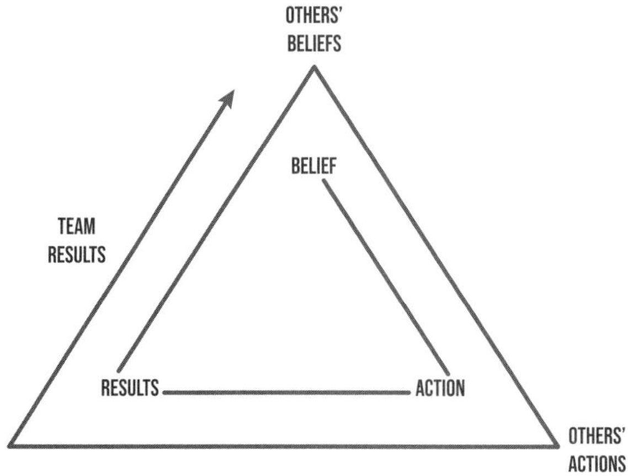

With the Trinity of Significance™, you first have to believe. Then you have to take the right action to get the right results. The results confirm that what you're doing is possible, which reinforces your belief in it, which leads to more action, which leads to more results. If you don't believe, you take little action, get few results, and start spiraling down a path that won't lead to transformation.

To get you started, we're anchoring you in that belief so you can start taking the action that leads to the results you're looking for by scaling your business. In order to take action to transform, you must believe it is possible. Average action will give you average results. Transformation is not an average result. In fact, most people will never reach it. With the odds against you, you've got to be all in, and the only way to take the extreme path that most won't is to fully believe this is possible for your life. Nobody "dabbles" their way to scale. It's done very intentionally. You have to go all in.

Be sure to go through this Section 2—Mindset—with your day-one mindset. I will talk about three things in this section:

- The difference between building a business of success and a business of significance
- What it means to clarify what you truly want for your business and your life
- How to get more done in less time

Are you ready for your next step toward unlimited growth, freedom, and joy?

3

SUCCESS VS. SIGNIFICANCE

I am an entrepreneur. I know how to build a business. The problem is that I don't have the vision for which steps I need to take in order to build in that way. If you show me the steps, I promise, I can create this.

— Top advisor

Chapter 3 Transformational Targets

- Exit the Red Line of Success™ and get on the Green Line of Significance™.
- Stop choosing between your lifestyle and your business.
- Stop chasing productivity alone and scale your business.

Many advisors are stuck in a rat race where productivity is directly tied to their time and effort. To earn more, they believe they have to work more. That mentality leads them to spend more and more hours in the office. Unfortunately, their peers in the industry praise these advisors for their increased production, which fuels them to push even harder every year. Nobody seems to realize the personal toll that takes on advisors and their families.

My father struggled with this very thing early on in his business. I remember as a kid wanting more of Dad's time, yet he always seemed to have one more call from a client who needed help. He didn't want to let them—or me—down. Business and life fought each other for his time. Dad had a difficult time finding a healthy and meaningful balance between the two. The interesting thing is that it takes success to get to the point where this is a problem. If you don't find a way to be successful, you won't have so many demands on your time. Many advisors never succeed in the first place. But as with a lot of things, sometimes the blessing of success leads to a curse if you aren't careful. This was the case for my dad for a lot of his career.

Many advisors—through trial and error—try to find a way to solve this. They look for answers but aren't equipped with the vision and steps required to change the course. And what they've done up to this point has worked so well that it's hard to change their direction. But as with anything, what got them here won't get them there. This represents the transformation from success to scale. While they struggle to solve this problem, they often lose hope altogether and just adopt the limiting mindset that "this is just the way it is," believing there is no other way.

Years ago, an advisor who was dealing with this made a very

interesting point. He said, "Shawn, I am an entrepreneur. I know how to build a business. The problem is that I don't have the vision for which steps I need to take in order to build that way. If you show me the steps, I promise I can create this."

To resolve this tension, some advisors turn to partnerships with other advisors. Usually that doesn't work because those advisors are mired in the same situation. Everyone is looking for a way to break the cycle and achieve scale without burnout, but few find it. Eventually, most lose hope and conclude that there simply is no other way to be successful.

They believe they must make a choice between business growth and personal freedom. They can have whichever they choose but never both at the same time. It's just the way it is. Why? Because most advisors have been taught that time and productivity are one and the same. Think about the beginning of your career—the more people you talked to, the more clients you got. Right? This ideal is ingrained in advisors' heads from day one, and it has worked, so it's hard to change later on in life. There's a direct relationship between business growth and personal freedom, something like a teeter-totter.

Productivity goes up, and your available time goes down. As you keep pushing more and more production, you see that your available time decreases. As you can see in the chart below, I call this the Red Line of Success™. That's where you experience success, but because it's tied to you, all your time is wrapped up in achieving it.

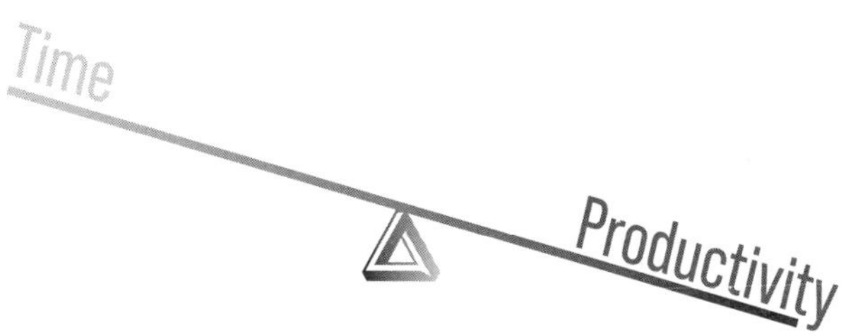

But there's another line—the line of significance, or scale. This is the Green Line. The Green Line leads to scale so you can lead a life of significance and **#DBDL**.

These are two vastly different approaches to growth.

Here is a side-by-side comparison that shows how they relate to your business.

The differences between the Red Line of Success™ and the Green Line of Significance™.

Which resonates with your current state?

Red Line (success)	**Green Line (significance)**
Success as productivity	Success as unlimited growth, freedom, and joy
Productivity is a function of time and effort	Productivity is a function of leveraging time
Business is primarily dependent on me	Business is less and less dependent on me
Unhealthy, unsustainable	Rejuvenating, sustainable
Low equity value, not sellable	Equity in business, highly marketable exit
Outcome: burnout or frustration	Outcome: freedom and enjoyment
Life of success	Life of significance
Finite game	Infinite game
Day-two mentality	Day-one mentality
Thinking like an advisor	Thinking like a business owner

Let's explore this concept further.

The Red Line of Success™

Like my dad and Anthony, most advisors start out in the business eager to take over the world. They don't have any clients or much demand on their time, so they have all the time in the world to produce and build their business. Productivity is low. But then as they grow, they start to produce, and as production goes up, demands on their time (service, business operations, etc.) increase (teeter-totter). Then the time they have available to produce decreases. With more success, there's more demand on their time, and the next thing you know, they have a full schedule and still have to produce, so they increase their hours so they can keep growing and surviving.

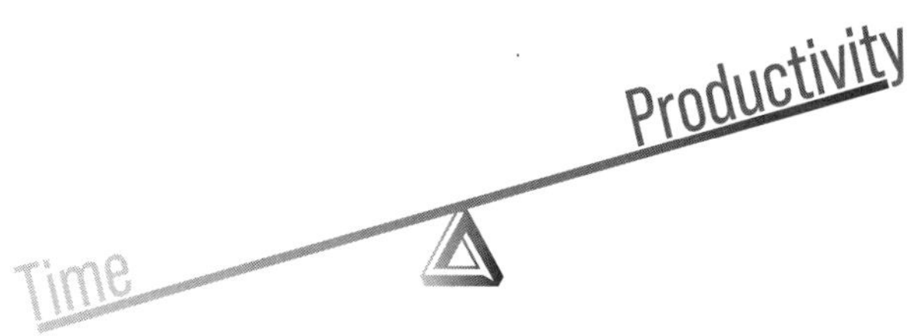

This way of working is a limiting way of thinking that will lead to one of only two destinations—stagnation or burnout.

Let's take that same way of thinking about time and productivity and picture it as a simple grid where the x axis indicates productivity and the y axis represents time. Once again, we see that productivity is a direct result of time worked. When one increases, so does the other. Work more hours; make more money. That's the line Anthony was following when he started looking for a third way. He worked as hard as or harder than anyone else, and

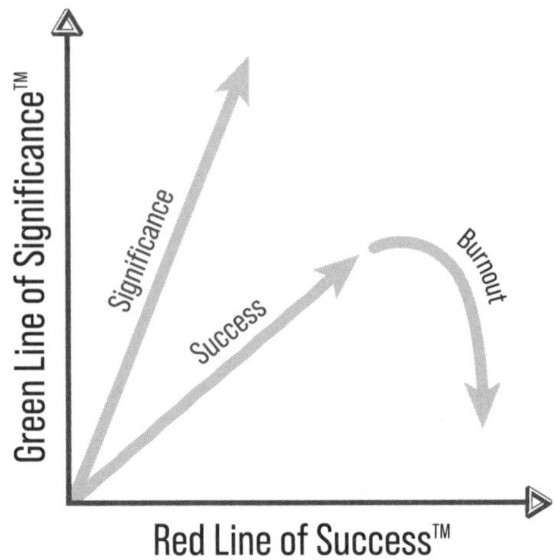

that drove the productivity in his business. So far, so good.

But you can only do what I call "riding the Red Line of Success" for so long before you run out of the one resource that's driving growth—your time. After all, there are only 168 hours in each week. Even if you spend every waking moment on your business, you'll eventually run out of the fuel that runs your company. That's the same fuel that powers the rest of your life, so you'll also be short on time for self-care, personal growth, rest, family, and other vital relationships. Riding the Red Line of Success all the way to the top eventually leads to a crash called burnout.

So why do so many advisors do it? Why can't they see it? Because when they're riding the Red Line—to some degree—they feel good about what they're doing. Being productive feels good. Knowing that you're making money for your family feels good. And when you get tired, unmotivated, or feel badly because you miss your kid's soccer game, you justify it by saying, "But I'm doing this for my family."

In reality, all your kids want is their mom or dad back.

Sadly, I've counseled countless advisors who didn't realize this until it was too late. They had thriving businesses, received lots of awards, and earned an amazing income. Yet their lives were unsustainable, eventually leading to a crash. The outcome was this: success with less freedom, lower quality of life, and less joy. Or, hoping to get their life back under control, they gave up on the growth of their business altogether. In that equation, they ended up not using their gifts to their full potential. They gave up.

Anthony knew that his current growth strategy—working more to produce more—was unsustainable. Yet he also knew that reducing his hours at work would curtail growth. He knew it had to be one or the other—business growth or personal satisfaction. So Anthony made the choice that I've seen many other advisors make. He decided to put the brakes on his business and invest more time in his personal life and family.

If you read between the lines, you'll see that they're really saying, "I wasn't able to grow my business and have a great life at the same time."

This is prime day-two mindset. You have worked hard in your career, and now you have "arrived" to where you no longer have to work anymore. You can focus on life and no longer choose to build or progress at all. Without progression, you are often left empty and unexcited for the future for the first time. It's like you've put your passion and purpose to sleep and are just going through the motions based on what is required of you. And if you aren't excited, it's contagious—your team won't be excited either. If you build a business you no longer want to be part of, you've probably built it wrong. The source is burnout, but it's disguised as success. Your business should be an enhancement to your overall life, not a trade-off. That is the whole point of *The Advisor Transformation* and **#DBDL**.

You do not have to choose between your lifestyle and the growth of your business if you build your business correctly.

If you build a business you no longer want to be part of, you've probably built it wrong.

While lifestyle advisors avoid burnout, they inevitably encounter an equally damaging crisis—stagnation. Entrepreneurs are wired for growth. They thrive when there's a fresh challenge and the growth line is moving up and to the right. Very few advisors can tolerate the boredom that comes from operating at a plateau, doing the same work every day, never facing fresh challenges, and never seeing the top line move up and to the right. Eventually, they wake up to the realization that they no longer love their work. I've seen advisors try to escape this completely. They sell their practices and enter a new career. To them, that feels like their only way out of the mayhem they've built. Then they start over and, if they succeed again, they arrive at the same place. Why not just build something right the first time? Think of the compound effect of that.

Burnout or stagnation are the only two stops on the Red Line. As long as you believe that your time is the one thing that can drive the success of your practice, you're bound to arrive at one or the other. But there is another way to think about growth. That means there's another way to organize your business. I call it the Green Line of Significance™.

The Green Line of Significance™

Your relationship with time and productivity is the key to the Green Line. Your time cannot be the driving factor in your productivity.

I've been fortunate to work with many of the most successful advisors in the country who have discovered the way to have both career success and personal satisfaction. Hitting goals they've never thought they could achieve, I've seen dreams come true. But the most rewarding achievement for me has been seeing lives change for the better once people have greater insight into and security concerning their finances. I have watched families free themselves from being overwhelmed by managing a demanding business to having time to travel, create memories, coach Little League games, and experience personal wins that otherwise wouldn't have been possible. And all that began with the simple, foundational realization that business growth is not directly connected to your time and effort. The Red Line doesn't offer a way to really grow your business. Real growth, the kind of growth that gives you freedom instead of making you a servant to the clock, is driven by scale. I call that the Green Line of Significance™.

Scale is a force multiplier because it multiplies what you can get done with your time. But scale is ultimately unrelated to the amount of time you spend working. Scale depends on adding personnel, systems, infrastructure, and leadership so your business grows without stretching your calendar. In fact, with scale, the growth of your business is completely unattached from your time and effort.

Sustainable growth is the result of building scale, not spending time. Green Line growth does not demand more and more of your energy. It actually requires less and less, giving you the freedom to invest in your family, yourself, your hobbies, and your interests. Ultimately, a business that scales will grow whether you're there or not.

There is no cap on Green Line growth. It does not stop when you stop working. It does not lead to burnout, and it does not lead to plateau. Red Line growth is always limited because your time is limited. But there is no limit on scale. Here's the comparison.

The intentional outcome of the Green Line:

1. Unlimited growth
2. Freedom
3. Joy

Compare this to the inevitable outcome of the Red Line:

1. Burnout
2. Stagnation

The Green Line = unlimited growth, freedom, and joy. That's the equation that works. When growth isn't capped because of your time and effort, then growth is unlimited. And as your business becomes more successful, you get more personal freedom. Finally, the more successful your business is the more fun it is to be part of it.

That is why scaling your business is the best outcome.

So what does it mean to build a business that scales? It's when a high-growth business and a lifestyle business intersect. There is no need to choose between having a growth business or a lifestyle

> So what does it mean to build a business that scales? It's when a high-growth business and a lifestyle business intersect. There is no need to choose between having a growth business or a lifestyle business.

business. You can have both. That's really the whole point of scale.

The benefit here is not that you won't work. It's that your business becomes less dependent on you over time. That gives you freedom. You will have the ability to work when you choose to do so. It also means that at some point, your work will not be required in order for your business to grow. It's easy to build a business that sustains itself when you are present. It may even sustain itself while you are gone, which means the needs of clients will be met in the short term. This isn't common, but it also isn't hard. It's much more difficult to have a business that grows while you are absent. And the prize is having a business that not only sustains but also grows when you are gone. When that happens, you'll have a business you love, one that doesn't feel like a job. A business that scales will bless your life as opposed to becoming your life.

People often define success by the amount of production they bring in or money they make. Unfortunately, this is not a sustainable motivator over time. Unless it's accompanied by increased freedom, earning more money will send you careening down the Red Line.

And (you may be experiencing this) the more success you gain, the less joy and happiness you actually have. That being said, if your business is set up to scale, you will reap the rewards of unlimited growth, which leads to more monetary success than you could ever gain on the Red Line. The more scalable your business is, the more financial upside and freedom you'll have.

So which do you prefer?

Get on the Green Line of Significance™!

Throughout the last seventeen years, I have obsessed over what it takes to be successful as a financial advisor. You might say I've been a student of the game. As a result, I have learned what it takes to build a business that scales. I know how to overcome common problems that advisors face and how to break old habits in order to achieve new, seemingly impossible goals. I've discovered how to help advisors grow professionally and personally so they, too, will experience the freedom to live the life they truly want. It's been gratifying to see them become better wives and mothers, better husbands and fathers, better versions of themselves, and more successful businesspeople.

I've coached many advisors who have done this. They have built businesses that scale beyond their wildest dreams and give them the freedom that they and their families deserve. They enjoy a business that has limitless potential and grows even while they're away. What's more, I've seen this transformation accomplished in as little as twelve months with the right guidance and clarity.

I believe every advisor has what it takes to scale if they have the right guidance and a step-by-step plan. I also believe it can be done in much less time than any of us ever thought possible. I've seen this over and over again, starting with my own father. His life—and my life—changed because of it.

That's why I wrote this book. I want to help you get your life back and build a scalable business. *The Advisor Transformation* is a blueprint for going from zero to scale in your business. It's a step-by-step guide to changing your thinking, aligning your focus, and building the infrastructure that will enable your business to thrive with less and less of your direct involvement. With this plan, you'll be able to scale your business sooner than you ever thought. And all of that can begin for you when you change your mindset. Do you believe this is possible for your business and life? Let's take the next step together.

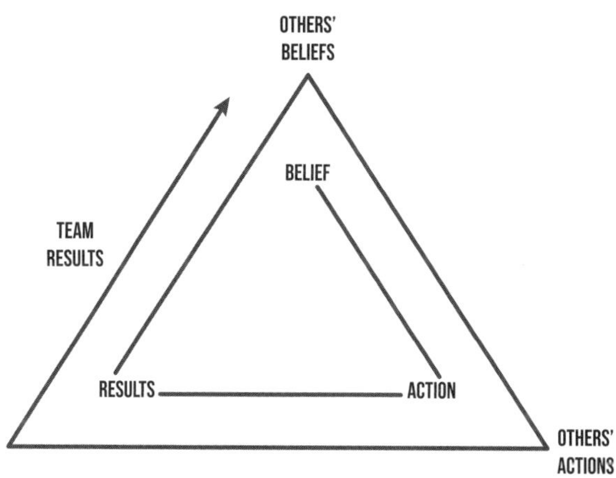

Chapter 3
Transformational Takeaways

- Many advisors are stuck in a rat race where productivity is directly tied to time worked.
- Riding the Red Line means chasing productivity and running a business where growth is dependent on your time.
- Riding the Red Line leads to burnout and stagnation.
- Running a lifestyle business means giving up a career you really like because you can't figure out how to have that career and live the lifestyle you want to live.
- You do not have to choose between your lifestyle and your practice.
- Riding the Green Line means refusing to chase productivity, which is tied directly to your time, and instead building a business that scales.
- Riding the Green Line leads to more growth, freedom, and joy in your business and in your life.

4

GETTING STARTED

Just a couple more years of this grind. Then I'll have the business where I need it, and I'll start enjoying my life.

— Top advisor

Chapter 4 Transformational Targets

- Start thinking like a business owner rather than an advisor.
- Identify your Enemies of Scale and commit to change.
- Transform through clarity, confidence, and capability.

When we met Anthony, he had reached a crisis point in his personal life. He had decided to scale back his success in order to put family first. About that time, Anthony met up with a friend, Derek, who is also a financial advisor. As they talked, Anthony realized that Derek had an even more successful business than his and had much more freedom. Derek's personal life wasn't out of balance. He had the time and energy to enjoy life and relationships. He took months off from his business each year, and the business kept growing without him.

"That was an eye-opening moment for me," Anthony said. "I realized that I'd learned the productivity part of the business but had totally missed the part about freedom. It was like I was working for the business instead of the business working for me, or that the business owned me instead of the other way around."

In that moment, Anthony made the decision that would change his business and his life forever. He decided to get on the Green Line and build a business that scales. He wouldn't have called it that at the time, but that's the choice he made. And he did more than make an intellectual choice; he took action. He had no other choice but to go all in and transform.

Not long after that conversation, Anthony took a trip to Massachusetts to spend a few days learning from Derek and his staff. Anthony became a student of the business again, but this time with a different goal. He wanted to learn how to scale his business, not just increase his own productivity. He set out to learn everything he could about how his friend had constructed and operated his business so he could grow the Green Line without pouring more and more hours into work. Anthony learned lessons about mindset, staffing, team leadership, and identifying high-leverage work. Most importantly, he learned that he had to stop thinking like a successful advisor and start thinking like a business owner.[5] This point became crystal clear when Derek asked Anthony, "If your business doubled from where it is today, on your current path, how would your life look? Could you handle it?" **#DBDL**

Anthony's answer: "No. Not at all."

Anthony decided that rather than trying to double his production, he'd grow the business so it was half as dependent on him. Ironically, advisors who make that decision unlock the key to growing their business way beyond what they could have done before.

So Anthony returned home and began implementing the strategies he'd learned.

Week by week, little by little, things started to fall into place. With each step he took toward thinking like a business owner rather than a successful advisor, Anthony felt more weight lift from his shoulders. It took courage at first to step away and give up control. But with each step, he became more and more confident

5 Remember, the #DBDL icons highlight scalable activities that will allow you to do business, do life.

that this would work for him. Within months, he was able to spend less time at work while continuing to see Green Line growth. Less than two years later, Anthony's business completely transformed. Check out how his business changed.

Actual Case Study: Total Production and How Much the Founding Advisor Was Responsible For

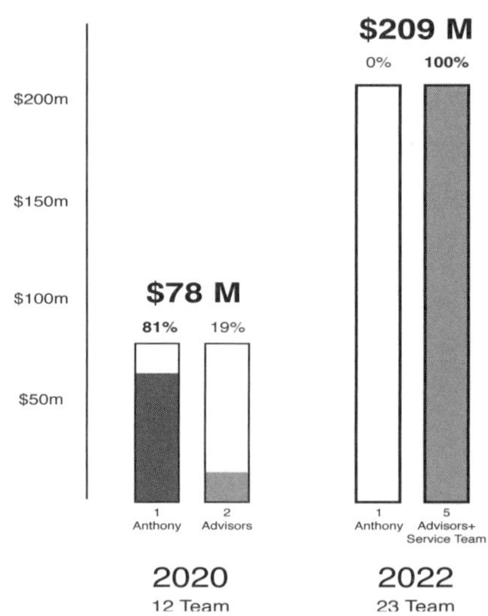

Anthony's business went from an advisory practice that had him tied to work like a ball and chain to a fully scalable business where productivity was no longer a function of Anthony's time. In fact, while I was writing this book, Anthony returned from a six-week vacation with his family. He didn't receive a single work call during that time. However, he did receive a few text messages from his team, highlighting their successes. He had requested these because he wanted them to stay motivated, and he wanted to enjoy the progress his team was making while he was away. He wanted to watch them grow while he was gone—such a sharp

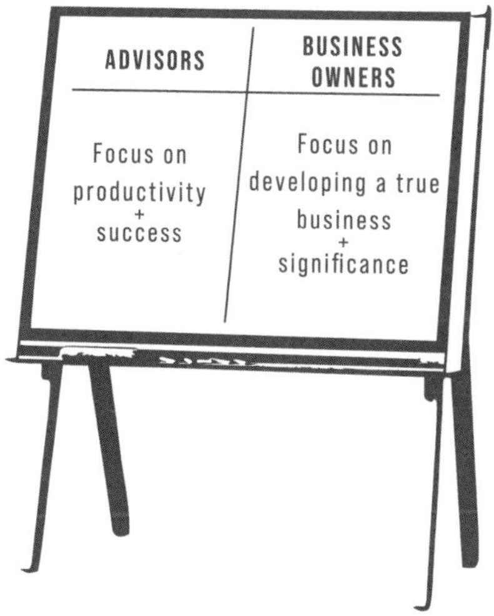

contrast to forcing his business to grow like before.

As for Anthony's family? They had fantasized about a vacation like that. And it became a reality just a few short years after Anthony changed direction. His wife also ended up with the husband she always knew Anthony could be, and the kids got a present father.

That's how real the possibility of scale is. If you know it's possible, learn how to do it, and make a commitment to build your business that way. I have seen advisors make huge strides in a few short months and make a complete transformation in less than a year. While that doesn't happen in every case, I can tell you that this transformation is absolutely possible if you pursue it with the same mindset you used to become successful in the first place, and if you go all in, you can achieve this. If you dabble, the dream will drift away day by day from ever becoming a reality.

Enemies of Scale: How and Why We Get in Our Own Way

It's possible you're thinking something like this: "I see what you're saying, but that just won't work for me." I hear some version of that nearly every time I speak to a group of advisors about scaling their business. These advisors have already realized that something needs to change in their business and in their life. They understand that the course they're on is not sustainable. Many have already tried to do something about it but have fallen victim to Enemies of Scale.

Enemies of Scale prevent scale from actually happening. These enemies come in all shapes and sizes. They may be a mindset, a lie that's told, or even a misstep in strategy. But the enemies will block progress and keep advisors on the Red Line.

Why Do Enemies of Scale Exist? Enemies of Scale exist in part because humans are resistant to change.

Helena Boschi, a psychologist who focuses on applied neuroscience in the workplace, explains it this way.

"It is difficult for the brain to change its plans. Even if we change our mind, it does not necessarily mean that we can change our behavior. Changing a behavior involves complex neural coordination among multiple brain areas, but if we do not do it quickly, it is often too late. The longer a decision stays in the brain, the harder it is to change it." [6]

When my daughter, Charlotte, was three, she broke her arm. The day it happened, she had to get a cast. "Daddy, I don't want a cast," she told me.

I said, "Well, you've got to get one or your arm is going to grow like this," and I put my arm at a weird angle. She got the cast, and everything was fine. Three weeks later, it was time to remove the cast.

"Are you excited to get your cast off?" I asked her.

6 https://welldoing.org/article/the-neuroscience-change-why-changing-course-painful-for-brain

"I don't want my cast off," she said.

That's how resistant the human brain is to change. Only three weeks earlier she didn't want to wear a cast, and now she had become so used to it that she didn't want to change back to the way things were.

Neuroscientists have studied how our brains react to change. Our brains hate it! When we change a habit (or thought pattern), the brain has to do more work, so it resists. Resisting change is your brain's natural reaction to doing less work. Your brain wants you to stay the course even though your heart tells you that you need to build in another way.

To scale, you must understand that what got you here won't get you there. You've got to push through that need to stay and get comfortable with change.

Common Enemies of Scale[7] SCALE

Below are some of the most common Enemies of Scale I see with advisors. Throughout the rest of *The Advisor Transformation*, I'll share many more Enemies of Scale (look for the icon).

SCALE *Resolving to make a change and never getting started.* This happens when advisors are excited to change but open their emails on Monday morning and realize they have a ton of work to do. They have absolutely no idea how to change their business model, so they go back to business as usual and by default drift back to the normal Red Line behavior.

SCALE *Rallying the team in hopes of spreading out the workload without providing clear direction.* Rallying your team around your vision is impossible to do without step-by-step

7 Remember, enemies of scale are the activities that will keep you from moving toward scale.

guidance on how to do it and why it matters to them.

Hiring new team members in the hopes that throwing people at the problems will fix them. Without arming your team with the proper processes and onboarding them to set them up for success, the problems won't go away.

Taking on a partner in hopes of spreading out the workload. When advisors take on a partner or hire a couple of random staff members to relieve some of the pressure on their time, those unguided hires are often ineffective and devolve the organization into a toxic work situation.

Shifting toward scale with a huge burst of enthusiasm and then giving up. This starts with an advisor who is full of energy and devotes a great deal of time and effort to scaling for several weeks or even months. But because they lack guidance, they accomplish little and eventually give up.

Failed attempts to change and move toward the Green Line can be disillusioning. These situations can leave the struggling advisor worse off than before, knowing that change is necessary but feeling utterly incapable of making it happen. Some advisors just keep plowing ahead until they eventually burn out. Others, like Anthony, make the reluctant choice to put their ambition in neutral and let their business stagnate.

It's obvious that you've gotten this far in *The Advisor Transformation* because you believe you need to transition to a business that will scale. You know you need your business to become less dependent on you, along with some of your key team members over time. The biggest reason people don't scale is because they don't know it's possible. They've built their business based on their own productivity and nothing else. They don't know

What got you here,
won't get you there.

any other way. But again, what got you here won't get you there.

To really transform, you've got to understand the Three Cs of Transformation™—clarity, confidence, and capability. In order to transform, you must first be clear on the direction and steps you need to take to transform. Once you are clear, you then will have confidence to take the action necessary to actually transform. Only then are you capable of transforming.

Most advisors stay on the same path until it's too late to do anything else. Have you heard the allegory about the frog in a kettle of water? At room temperature, the frog is perfectly fine. As the heat is turned up a degree or two, the frog gets a little warm but is still okay. Not feeling the gradual change, the frog stays in the kettle until the water boils. By then, it's far too late to make an escape. Had the frog jumped straight into the boiling water, it would have immediately jumped out—YIKES! But because the process was done little by little, the frog ended up boiling.

This is much like advisors on the Red Line. Had the advisors just woken up living in a Red Line business, they would have said, "No, this isn't right for me." But because the problem was gradual, it snuck up on them, and they didn't think to take an immediate corrective action and didn't know how. So they just keep going, maybe even thinking if they work harder they can work their way out of the problem. But day by day they create a bigger problem until their life and free time have completely boiled away.

Anthony was the frog in the kettle. He had just about reached the boiling point when he went into the bathroom, rinsed off his face, and said, "I'm done." It took rock bottom for him to realize that he had to take the necessary actions in order to change.

Fortunately, he spoke with his good friend Derek who, showed him another way.

That's how Anthony began to develop a different vision for the future of his business, his teammates, and his family. That moment of awareness changed everything for him. He couldn't get out of the boiling kettle until he knew that something else was possible.

Anthony had to have vision to get on the Green Line, and so do you. You must be able to envision a different business, a different future, and a different outcome for your work and your personal life. That means shifting your focus from being an advisor to being a business owner. That means moving from focusing on productivity alone to developing a true business.

Why You've Got to Go All In

Anthony's story is a great example of what can happen when you get on the Green Line. Let's look at an advisor who stayed on the Red Line.

Jeff was an incredible, highly productive financial advisor. The business he built was applauded by all his peers and envied by nearly everyone. He had more than $500 million on the books and produced a solid income for himself. Yet when he went home each day to his family, he realized he was sacrificing a lot. He had missed far too much time with his children when they were young. His life revolved around his business, not the other way around. Jeff was riding the Red Line, although he didn't realize it at the time.

As the years passed, Jeff reached the inevitable point of burnout. Yet he told himself, "Just a couple more years. I'll save up and be set for life. Then I can slow down and enjoy my life." A couple years went by, and he continued to tell himself, "Just a couple more years," not even realizing his stop date was a moving target. He just needed a little more time and a little more and a little more.

One day, Jeff told me, "Shawn, the amount of success you get is directly correlated to the amount of stress you can handle."

Tying your "success" to the amount of brute force and stress you can manage is an incorrect mindset. Handling more and more stress isn't sustainable. Do not adopt this mentality. Your success should equate to less stress over time, not more. #DBDL

Jeff pushed himself and continued to pursue success. Jeff's family, however, didn't want to live like that or wait for Jeff to figure it out. His wife divorced him, and his kids grew up and moved on. He walked into his home office one evening and looked at the sales awards, trophies, and plaques he'd accumulated over the years. Tears trickled down his face. The pride he had while earning them no longer mattered. Those trophies no longer represented accomplishments. Instead, they were a reminder of the many years he'd wasted chasing things much less important than significance. They were like receipts of wasted time and life lost. What had he done?

At that moment, Jeff decided to make the change he'd been working toward all those years. He determined to sell his business and finally start living the life he'd wanted for so long. Within the industry, it was well known that Jeff had a large clientele and produced a terrific income, so he was convinced that his business

> Tying your "success" to the amount of brute force and stress you can manage is an incorrect mindset.

was very valuable and that he would receive sizable offers when he decided to sell it.

That didn't happen. Instead, would-be buyers realized that even though the business had a large number of accounts, every client was tied to Jeff personally. It was by no means certain that Jeff's clients would be as loyal to a new advisor as they had been to him. No one was willing to risk a large sum on the purchase of a business that was tied to one person who would be leaving the office. Some offers did come, but in every case, the would-be buyers wanted Jeff to ensure the loyalty of his clients by remaining in the business for three more years—as their employee. To get a reasonable price, Jeff would have to become a hired hand in the very business he had sacrificed so much to build. Jeff simply couldn't make himself do it. But he was too burned out to stay. So he sold the business for a fraction of its value and moved on. The sale of Jeff's business was one of the quickest transactions I've ever seen. He was burned out and clearly said, "Enough is enough. Just take this business. I want my life back."

That's a sad story, one that plays out far too often in our business. The financial services industry is one of the most powerful avenues I know for creating unlimited growth and freedom for financial advisors, their families, and their clients. But for many, this business

> "Enough is enough. Just take this business. I want my life back."

becomes a burden that produces constant tension in the advisor's life. It's the tension between building a profitable business and living a life of meaning and purpose. I've seen this over and over among my coaching clients. That's life on the Red Line.

Had Jeff been on the Green Line, he would have been able to sell a business that wasn't dependent on him. He would have built significant equity in his business. Most people get an earnout, not a buyout. They sell their company and then become an employee for someone else for three to five years. While they stay on, they no longer have control over making important decisions about marketing, who to hire, and so on. And if the business doesn't reach the financial metrics dependent on the earnout, the sale price is actually reduced. So you sell your business, gain a boss, lose control, and your performance determines how much money you actually get in the end. Yes, it's a sad story.

If you want meaningful success, choose the Green Line, and choose it early. At some point, you will arrive at the destination you have chosen for yourself and your business. If you follow the Red Line, you'll burn out or plateau. It won't matter where you want to be. Those are the only two stops on that line. You will wind up at one or the other. To change that trajectory, you must make a choice. It's impossible to build a scalable business by doing the same things you've always done.

You already have two of the three foundations needed to build a scalable business—vision and guidance. You know it's possible. You have an initial vision for scale, which we'll refine in the next section, Section 3. And you have the guidance you need—*The Advisor Transformation*—to make that vision a reality. Finally, you know you've got to commit to going all in. Your job is massive action! Follow these foundations, and you will ride the Green Line all the way to freedom.

The only question now is whether you're ready to commit yourself to this transformation. What are you going to do when you close this book and then Monday happens and life starts coming at you like a cannonball? The urgent will always trump the important if you let it. Don't let it. Trust the process, and follow it through.

The urgent will always trump the important if you let it. Don't let it. Trust the process, and follow it through.

The truth is that you will never be closer to the Green Line than you are today. With every day that passes, more problems and complications appear. That's life. The things we thought we would do when the time was right or when things slowed down a bit inevitably move farther and farther out of reach. That's what happened to my friend Jeff. By the time he made the choice to switch to the Green Line, it was too late. The opportunity had disappeared.

Will you go all in? I truly hope so. But here's a test. The majority of books are never finished. Readers give up before they reach the end. Be the exception by reading this one completely so you can increase the chances that you will build a business to scale.

Chapter 4
Transformational Takeaways

- To get off the Red Line and onto the Green Line, you have to start thinking like a business owner, not an advisor.
- Enemies of Scale exist in part because humans are resistant to change.
- Enemies of Scale include:
  - Resolving to change without actually starting
  - Rallying your team without clear direction
  - Taking on a partner to spread the workload without clear direction
  - Hiring new staff in the hopes that throwing people at problems will fix them
  - Shifting toward scale and then giving up too soon
- The Three Cs of Transformation™ are clarity, confidence, and capability.

5

LEVERAGE IS EVERYTHING

Give me a place to stand, and a lever long enough, and I will move the world.

— Archimedes

Chapter 5 Transformational Targets

- Save money, time, and energy by learning how to leverage people, technology, and capital.
- Eliminate the idea that if you want something done right, you have to do it yourself.
- Understand the three primary constraints in your business—time, quality, and cost—and how to work with them.

As you think about your business, do you think like an advisor or like a business owner? Your answer will reveal a lot about the decisions you make every day and will determine where your business will most likely end up. To put it plainly, advisors who think like advisors usually stay on the Red Line. Advisors who begin to think like business owners tend to move to the Green Line. There's a simple reason for that.

As we've seen, most advisors approach their work believing that business growth happens in direct relation to their investment of time. The more they work, the more they earn. It's a brute-force method of growing a business. The productivity of the business will always correlate to the effort the advisor exerts. That's our teeter-totter. Time and productivity have exactly the same weight. When one goes up, the other goes down in direct proportion, and vice versa.

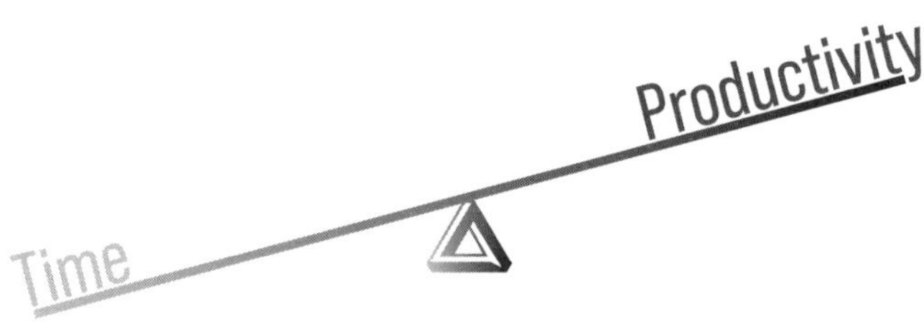

Business owners think differently, especially when it comes to their time. They realize their time is very limited, so they are constantly looking to get more done in less time. They want a greater return on their time. We call that leverage. Leverage, by its essence, embodies the principle of achieving heightened outcomes with diminished effort. Think of a teeter-totter. Imagine placing a heavy weight on one end of the teeter-totter. Attempting to lift it with mere manual effort can be both taxing and time-consuming.

However, by simply applying a modest force to the opposite end using the seesaw's pivot point, you can effortlessly elevate the heavy weight. Here, the seesaw acts as a tool of leverage, enabling you to achieve a task with significantly less energy and time.

This is the magic of leverage—accomplishing more with less. Just as the seesaw amplifies our strength, in the realm of business and life, the right tools, strategies, and methods can magnify our results, allowing us to reach our objectives more efficiently and effectively.

Virgin Group founder Richard Branson is a great example of someone who accomplishes more with less. Branson owns more than 400 companies. Even if he worked every day of the year, he couldn't devote even one day to each business. Yet they're all running successfully. How does he do it? By harnessing the principle of leverage. Branson is a business owner. He's not an entrepreneur who works in a business. He has businesses and builds them to where their productivity is not based on his sweat equity. By spending even a single hour on a project, he's been able to multiply the impact of that time.

Greek physicist Archimedes was the first to articulate the principle of leverage. He once said, "Give me a place to stand, and a lever long enough, and I will move the world." His point was clear: with leverage, there's no limit to what you can do. It is a critical factor of scale and can produce unlimited output. With the right leverage, you can lift a car with little effort or scale your business by ten, fifty, or a hundred times its current value while spending less and less of your energy over time.

To scale your business, you must understand the principle of leverage. You cannot scale by brute force. You must look for ways to amplify the use of your resources, especially your most valuable resource—you. This is the critical shift you must make in your thinking in order to move from the Red Line to the Green Line. You must stop thinking like an advisor and start thinking like a business owner.

Stop trying to scale your business by investing more and more time in it. Start looking for ways to leverage your time, energy, ideas, and money in order to produce a greater impact than you could have achieved based on your effort alone. That begins with understanding the three main forms of leverage in the financial services business. Here are the primary levers you have to work with:

- Human capital
- Technology
- Financial capital

Leverage Human Capital

Back in the misty age when dinosaurs roamed the Earth, there lived an enterprising caveman named Og. Over the years, Og developed a reputation among his fellow cave dwellers for hard work and strength. Og was a big guy, a prehistoric Arnold Schwarzenegger, and his specialty was moving big boulders. When someone had a boulder stuck in the entrance to their cave or one blocking the path to a water hole, Og was the go-to guy. With one swift motion, he hugged the stone to his chest, pushed it over his head, and walked it to the rock pile. Og was simply the best in the business at moving big rocks. And the best part? For every boulder he moved, Og was paid one cave buck, enough to buy a quarter pound of brontosaurus steak or two whole cassava roots. Sometimes, Og could move twelve or thirteen boulders a day. His brute strength made him one of the most prosperous cavemen in the entire glacial valley.

One day, Og's neighbor, a young caveman named Trog, asked if he could help move boulders. Trog was a strapping young lad, so Og didn't doubt that he could move big rocks. But Og was reluctant to split his profits. And he couldn't be sure Trog wouldn't drop a boulder on somebody's foot. Supervising Trog would only take time away from Og's moving boulders and there was no guarantee that even with supervision, helping Trog would help Og's business. Besides that, Og was used to doing everything himself, and that's the way he liked it.

However, the boulders were really heavy. Og ended each day exhausted, miserable, and sore. Sometimes, he had to take a few days off to recover before moving any more boulders. After a while, Og realized he could only move about ten boulders a day before he became totally exhausted. That was the limit of his energy.

Sound familiar?

At last, Og realized he needed help and agreed to hire Trog on a trial basis. "I'll give you fifty cave cents for every boulder you move," Og said.

"It's a deal," Trog replied. He'd never dreamed of making up to five cave bucks in a single day.

As it turns out, Trog did a great job moving boulders. After six months, Trog was moving more boulders than Og was. By hiring just one caveman, Og had more than doubled his business. And since he was only paying Trog half the boulder-moving fee, Og's income had gone up by 50 percent. So Og asked Trog if he had any friends who could move rocks. Before long, Og had hired Grog as the third caveman on the boulder crew. Grog was even stronger than Trog, so production went up even more. All together, they moved at least thirty-five boulders a day. And if one of them missed a day, productivity was still double what it had been when Og worked alone.

One day it dawned on Og that the younger cavemen were much better at moving boulders than he was. Og realized his best skill was lining up work from other cavemen. He still had a reputation as the best rock mover in the valley, and everyone trusted his crew because Og had vouched for them. But Og was ready to spend more time with his family and less time at work. He was burned out carrying boulders, but he also didn't want his business to stagnate. So Og stopped moving boulders, let his crew move the boulders, and spent his time among his cave neighbors finding out who needed a boulder moved and put somewhere else. Lots of them did, so Og soon hired three more cavemen, Bog, Chog, and Plog.

Within a year, Og had gone from moving ten boulders a day all by himself to having five team members who were able to move up to sixty boulders a day. Most days, Og never touched a rock, but he still brought in sixty cave dollars, and he paid half of that to his helpers. Og was now making three times the money he'd made a year before, but he was working far less. When he wasn't visiting caves to find new customers, Og spent most of his time with his cavewoman, Mog, and their little brood of cave children, Eek, Beek, Creek, and Deek. The next summer, Og was able to take his cave family on vacation at the salt flats to watch dinosaur races.

In this simple story, our caveman hero discovered the power of leverage. He went from thinking like a boulder mover to thinking like a business owner. He realized he could find people who needed their boulders moved much more quickly than he could move boulders. So the best use of his time was to prospect for new customers. Other people could move the rocks and were happy for the work. And Og made more money than he ever could have made on his own.

#DBDL

This is the power of leveraging human capital. It lets you accomplish more in less time. You also benefit from the skills of people who are often better equipped to do the actual labor than you are. In this example, overall daily output increased six times. As simple as this sounds, leveraging human capital is one of the most critical components of scale.

Although we've advanced well beyond the caveman, some advisors make the same mistake that Og did at first, growing their business on their strength alone. They look at teammates as an expense to the business as opposed to an asset that will fuel growth. And many advisors won't give up control of tasks that others can certainly do, sometimes even more efficiently. They think, "If I want something done right, I have to do it myself." That mentality is an Enemy of Scale. It limits the potential of your business to the time and energy of just one person—you.

Here's the mindset of a business owner. Never do something yourself that someone else can do for you. With that mindset, you'll stay securely on the Green Line. Your time is a limited resource. Your success depends on how efficiently and effectively you use your time. If you use your time only to move rocks, an hour of your time will always be worth the value of one rock. Leverage your time by not doing things others can do and only doing things that fall within your unique abilities.

Here's the mindset of a business owner. Never do something yourself that someone else can do for you.

Leverage Technology

The second way to create leverage in your organization is through technology. By the power of technology, we can design systems that work automatically. Once established, these systems require no manual effort whatsoever. That may sound too good to be true, but the truth is that you're already leveraging technology to automate some of the things you do. The secret to scale is to use technology to automate every bit of work that you can. If a task can be done by a machine as well or better than by a human, there's no reason for you or anyone on your team to do it.

Consider this scenario. Many years ago, many of the advisors I worked with handwrote the notes they took during client meetings. Then they handed the notes off to an assistant. It was an old-school process that didn't work that well. Sometimes the assistant couldn't read the advisor's handwriting, sometimes the notes got misplaced, and so on. Even if the assistant could read the notes, they had to type them, send them back to the advisor, and then save them. From there, they created emails, follow-up reminders, and such. Now, advisors can use a voice dictation system. Not only does that eliminate the process that used to occur between assistant and advisor, but it also segments the notes exactly as you want them segmented, emails those notes to your key staff so they can provide deliverables, and uploads them to your customer relations manager. Can you imagine how much time that saves?

How much leverage does that create? If that advisor has a staff of three and those meetings involve four people for about ninety minutes, that's six hours of effort every week. At the nominal rate of $50 per hour for an average compensation, it would cost that advisor nearly $16,000 a year to manually record those meetings and respond to the client needs that come from them. And what

> *"AI is a machine's ability to perform the cognitive functions we associate with human minds."*
>
> —McKinsey & Company[8]

is the bonus? These automations can happen while your team is conducting meetings or spending time with their families.

Leveraging technology allows you to keep business moving independently of you. It doesn't require anybody to use their time or even lift a finger to make it happen. That's the power of leveraging technology.

Artificial Intelligence (AI)

Artificial intelligence (AI) is one of the most effective ways that technology enhances what humans can already do.

Advisors use AI to:

- Take notes through speech recognition.
- Create the framework for presentations. These tools allow you to enter what you want in your presentation as well as the audience that you're gearing it to and then create the outline for you.
- Create or edit content. This saves a lot of time and can be really helpful when you're stuck with what to say.

Tech tools can also help with planning. You can literally put

8 https://www.mckinsey.com/featured-insights/mckinsey-explainers/what-is-ai

a client's tax return into a tech software, and it will identify key findings and how to optimize for fewer taxes later. These types of tools are really valuable and help save a lot of time.

Creating leverage through technology does require an investment of time and, depending on which platforms you use, money. After all, a technological system can be a whole lot of work to build on the front end. That's why it must be seen as an investment and not an expense. A good tech solution will deliver returns for months, even years into the future. Aside from occasional system maintenance and refreshing content, it can work as designed indefinitely. Wouldn't that be worth some effort on the front end?

Think of it this way. If I told you that if you did 1,000 pushups this week you would be physically fit forever, would you do it? You might have to do ten pushups once a year or so, just to keep your edge. But there would be no more killer sessions at the gym—ever. My guess is that however long it took, you would get those 1,000 reps, knowing that the hard work you'd be doing this week will benefit you far into the future. Investing in technology has the same value for scaling your business. It can be a little painful in the short term, but the long-term benefits are exponential. And if you have the right partners to help you, the process will be much easier than you think. A business owner sees the long-term benefit of leveraging technology. Some advisors see it as a short-term headache. Which do you see?

Leverage Financial Capital

In every business there are three primary constraints: time, quality, and cost. When you increase one of those elements, one or more will have to decrease. So the general rule is that you can have any two of them in good measure, but not all three at the same time.

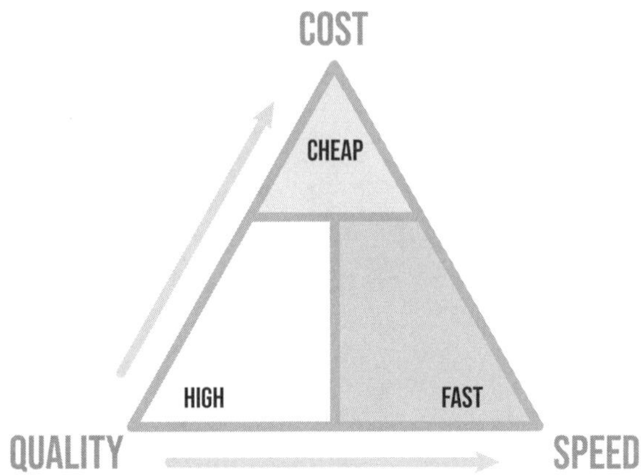

For example, you can complete a project very quickly and at a low cost if you want to. But you'll have to sacrifice quality in order to achieve that. Or you could have a high-quality, low-cost project, but it would take forever to complete. No matter what you're doing, those three constraints must be accounted for. That leads us to a third source of leverage in business—financial capital. If you have capital to spend and you can afford to pay a high price in order to get high-quality work done quickly, money really does buy time.

Financial capital allows you to scale quickly without sacrificing quality. If you can expand the financial side of your Iron Triangle, you will not have to sacrifice either of the other two. Financial capital also provides great leverage in assembling a team. With capital, you can build and assemble a high-performance team much faster than waiting for organic revenue to grow to the point of supporting them. Silicon Valley startups know this as do investors. They raise money in the multi-millions in order to afford the best talent and accelerate the speed at which the business can build. They may have no operating revenue, but they hire thirty teammates and pay them with borrowed capital. That allows them to advance to the revenue stage very rapidly.

One of the advisors I coach did something similar. Because he had capital, he was able to hire ten teammates the moment he opened his business. He did that with confidence, knowing that he had the means to afford it and that by doing so he could speed up the process of assembling the team and infrastructure prior to the organic growth he needed. He was thinking in terms of scale from the very beginning. As a result, he accomplished in twelve months what most companies take three to five years to achieve by relying on organic growth in order to fund the business.

#DBDL

Many offices must grow their revenue before they are able to hire. That means that by the time their business grows and the revenue is there, they have to hurry up and train new people. If you have the luxury of capital, you can hire before the growth so new teammates are well trained and running full speed ahead when you need them to contribute. Capital allows you to invest forward without necessarily having the revenue to satisfy it. We'll touch on that later.

Change the Game

Let's come back to the basic mechanics of leverage for a moment. You don't need to be a mechanical engineer to see that one of the models below provides great leverage and one doesn't. That's obvious. But what accounts for the difference?

The only difference between the two is the placement of the fulcrum, the pivot point for the lever. Move the fulcrum in the right direction, and you gain leverage. On a teeter-totter, that's a very simple adjustment to make. The same is true in your business. There are simple adjustments you can make right now that will begin to produce leverage in your business. These adjustments relate to human capital, technology, and financial capital.

As you become more accustomed to thinking like a business owner, you'll see and seize more and more leverage opportunities. In fact, I'd go so far as to say that this is the basic difference between thinking like an advisor and thinking like a business owner. Advisors tend to be doers, like Og the caveman. They're accustomed to moving things by brute force. Owners think in terms of leverage. They look for ways to multiply force through human capital, technology, and financial capital. They think about long-term benefits, not just short-term costs. They use leverage to their advantage.

Leverage is a powerful and fundamental tool for scaling your business because it provides what you and your business most need—more time. Leverage allows you to optimize your time and your teammates' time so everyone gets more with less effort. If you want to scale your business, you must understand leverage and use it to your advantage. Human capital, technology, and financial capital—these are the three levers you can use to scale your business. Use them well, and your business will begin to scale right now, starting today.

CHAPTER 5
TRANSFORMATIONAL TAKEAWAYS

- Thinking like a business owner rather than an advisor means using leverage to get a greater return on your time.
- There are three main forms of leverage in the financial services business:
    - Human capital
    - Technology
    - Financial capital
- Human capital allows you to benefit from the skills of people who are often better equipped to do the actual labor than you are while freeing up your time.
- Using technology to automate systems can save dozens of hours per week.
- Financial leverage allows you to do things more quickly than you might have otherwise.
- Every business has three primary constraints: time, quality, and cost.
- A huge Enemy of Scale is the mentality that if you want something done right, you have to do it yourself.

Looking to set your mindset for scale? Check out additional resources here.

SECTION 3
VISION

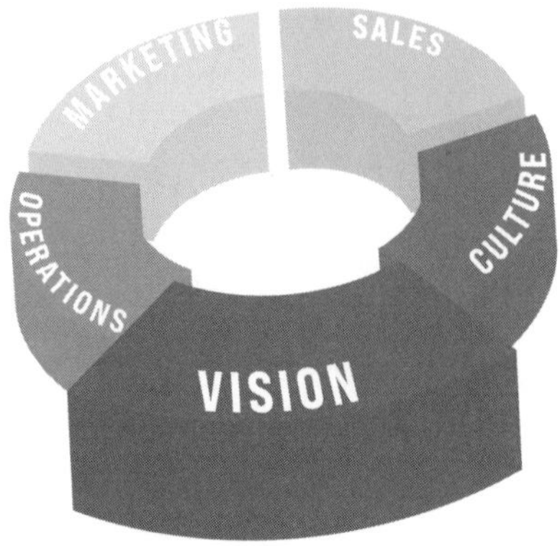

Your vision is the heartbeat of your business. It's the magnetic force that draws in the best talent and ignites passion in everyone who interacts with your brand. A compelling vision is the difference between a business that merely exists and one that thrives with purpose.

Show me your vision, and I will show you how it directly relates to the quality of people your business attracts and the enthusiasm they have for your business.

Show me your vision, and I will show you how it directly relates to the quality of people your business attracts and the enthusiasm they have for your business. Great people want to work for a business that has an exciting vision to do big things. And when they believe in it fully, they will do everything they can to bring it to life and share that vision with everyone—your clients, future employees, and community.

Imagine interviewing someone who wants to work for you. When they ask, "Where's the company headed?" your response is, "Eh, well I'm hoping to retire in a few years. Beyond that, I'm not really sure, but we are proud of what we've done." Who wants to work for a company like that? No one does, especially not top talent.

That is why vision comes first in Triad's 5 Principles to Scale™. Your vision bleeds into everything you do. It is the way you see the future in all aspects of your business.

A vision delves deeper than mere objectives. It answers the profound question, "Why does our company exist?" It's the lifeblood that brings your mission to life. Your vision must be exciting. It has to be something that not only you but your entire organization can look forward to. It's your just cause—your reason for getting up in the morning—and should feel like part of your DNA. It's not a statement that sits stagnant on a piece of paper. It's all of you. It's why you go to work. It's why you have a team. It's what you do, and it needs to be evident everywhere your team and your brand show up.

A vision delves deeper than mere objectives. It answers the profound question, "Why does our company exist?" It's the lifeblood that brings your mission to life.

When we created Triad, we had a vision to help our advisors get more growth, freedom, and joy in both their businesses and their lives. And once we settled on that vision, it became part of everything we do. We are so passionate about our vision that we want the idea of doing business and doing life to be contagious by anyone our company impacts, not just in our industry but throughout the country. To us, doing business and doing life means building a business of significance that 100 percent supports the lifestyle we want to live. That is why you may have noticed our DBDL on our social accounts. We are all about DBDL in everything we do because it supports our vision.

We exist in what is known as the Attention Economy, which means that the biggest commodity out there is people's attention. Each of us receives an average of 6,000 messages per day. Our brains filter these unless there's a compelling reason to keep paying attention. In the Attention Economy, your vision, which becomes your brand, is the only chance you have to stand out from your competitors. So not only does vision give you a purpose and attract new talent, but it also attracts customers.

So what's your vision?

If you don't have one, don't worry. This is what this section is all about. In it, we will talk about:

- Crafting a compelling vision.
- The transformational power of a clear vision.
- How it fuels everything you do—operations, sales, marketing, culture.
- Strategies to bring your vision to life.
- How to reinforce your vision with a strong ongoing foundation.

Are you ready for your next step toward unlimited growth, freedom, and joy? Let's dive in.

6

EVERYTHING FOLLOWS VISION

If he doesn't change something soon, he's going to work himself to death.

— Wife of a top advisor

Chapter 6 Transformational Targets

- Create a vision that is a long-term goal toward what you really want to do with your business.
- State your why, think through your growth plan, and rebuild the foundation of your business.
- Use your vision to help create systems that will scale your business.

Whenever I meet with an advisor for the first time, I start the conversation with this question: "As you think about the future of your business, what are you trying to build?"

This catches most advisors off guard.

Remarkably, most advisors have no clarity on the outcome they're after.

After a brief pause, they often say something like this: "I don't know. I've never really thought about it" or "A successful one" or something equally vague like a production number they want to achieve—"$1 billion in AUM.“ In other words, they simply don't know what they're trying to accomplish, let alone know how they are going to get there.

Given the varied array of businesses in the financial advice space, it's obvious that you can build whatever kind of business you want. I've seen so many different versions of success in this industry that it would be impossible to pinpoint what success looks like for everyone. As long as you are clear about what you want, you can find the right steps to create it.

Since you're still reading *The Advisor Transformation*, you have a desire to scale your business into an operation that will increase your financial potential and freedom at the same time. But let's go a little deeper. What is the true vision of your company? What do you want it to look like three years from now? Five years? Think into the future.

Vision is not a short-term aim; it's a long-term goal. That is one reason so many people struggle with it. People often overestimate what they can do in the short term and underestimate what they can do in the long term. If you build a long-term, incredible vision, don't be surprised by what you'll accomplish. Here are a few questions to ask yourself about your future business:

- How will your infrastructure need to evolve in order for you to scale?
- Who will you have to hire and in which key positions will you have to hire them in order to mature your business beyond you?
- Do people really know you and your company? Do your brand and message resonate with them?
- What do you want your business to be known for?
- What should your culture look like and mean to your teammates?
- What processes will need to be developed in order for your company to scale?
- What are the characteristics of your ideal client and what are the common problems you can help them with?
- How are you going to attract more of your ideal clients?

Answering these questions is how you create vision because vision is a clear picture of the future you are working to create. So again, what are you trying to create? What is your vision? If you're still saying, "I'm not sure," that's okay. As I mentioned, most advisors have not thought this question all the way through. The purpose of this section is to help you do that and arrive at an exciting vision for your company that will guide you over the next three to five years. It's to help you see what the Green Line looks like for you. If you don't have that yet, you soon will.

First, let's look at the power of creating vision. Then we'll give you our criteria for approaching vision. They include:

- Rethinking your vision for growth

- Stating your why
- Rebuilding your foundation

The Power of Vision

You probably know someone who "accidentally" created a successful business by doing the right things and getting good at their craft. In fact, that may describe your career as an advisor up to this point. With strong ability and hard work, you can achieve quite a bit. In fact, that's essentially what Red Line growth is. Scale is different. I've never seen anybody accidentally create a business that scales. Scale requires intentionality. To scale your business, you have to know where you're going. If you don't, the business will pick a destination for you.

Think of it like going for a run. Let's say you're on a run at a state park. You've heard there's a beautiful lake in the park, and you'd like to see it. You're also interested in adding to your mileage for the week, so you're hoping to get in at least five miles while overlooking the awesome view of the water.

As you take to the path, you're a bit worried about tripping over a root or rock, so you spend a lot of time looking at your feet. Because you're not exactly sure where the lake is, you simply pick a direction and begin jogging, rarely looking up ahead. After an hour or so, you realize that you've covered the same ground several times, and you still haven't caught sight of the lake. Since you forgot to hit the start button on your smartwatch, you're not exactly sure how far you've run. And now you're totally exhausted, too tired to keep looking for the lake. You take the trail back to the parking lot and head home.

That's what it's like to build a business without a clear vision. You have a vague destination in mind, but since you don't know precisely where you're trying to go, you aren't sure how to get there. Besides that, your eyes are glued to the ground, consumed with the day-to-day details of running the business. Because you never look ahead, you don't make the intentional progress needed to get you to the destination you desire. It doesn't matter how hard you run or how determined you are. Without clarity in the vision, you won't make the progress you want to make. Exhausted, you finally call it quits. That is how Red Line businesses work. There's no clear goal, just a frenzy of activity. SCALE

Without clarity in the vision, you won't make the progress you want to make.

Now, imagine the scenario differently. You'd like to get in a good run and see the lake. You've seen a map of the park, so you know the lake lies to the west. From the map, you've identified specific milestones and markers that will help keep you on your path as you run. You start in the right direction. There are some obstacles on the path, but by keeping your head up and eyes forward, you're able to navigate around them and confirm you are on the right track and making progress. After half an hour, you find yourself resting beside a beautiful body of water. After relaxing for a few moments, you feel refreshed enough to continue your run, and you complete a total of five miles.

That's the difference vision makes. Vision is looking down range toward a definite goal. It gives you a clear direction to pursue

#DBDL

and a way to measure progress. You should clearly see milestones and the steps needed to reach them while also measuring progress beyond production. It moves you in the right direction and much more quickly than you imagined. Because you know your destination and take intentional steps toward it, you wind up with the margin for other important things as well. That's the power of vision. The clearer it is, the more likely you are to reach the destination.

On the other hand, without a clear vision, running fast and hard day in and day out won't get you closer to your goal no matter how hard you try. In fact, effort won't get you to the lake. It may actually take you farther from it.

I've found that everything follows vision. Like a motorcycle, a business will move in whichever direction the rider looks. Turn your head to the right, and the bike will go right whether you want it to. Focus your efforts on client acquisition, and that's the direction your business will move. Focus on profit, and you'll move toward profit. Focus on scale, and you'll scale. That's how powerful vision is. Whatever you focus on will become your destination. Choose your focus wisely so you will be happy where you end up.

Wisdom is knowing how your short-term actions impact your long-term future. As humans, we are very shortsighted. Day to day we do what needs to be done in that moment. Because we don't look up, we end up in places we never intended. By having a clear vision, we have clarity . We are clear on where we want to end in the long term, and we can then backtrack to determine the steps we need to take in order to get there. This foresight guides us and ensures that we get closer to our desired future.

One of the greatest immediate benefits to having a long-term

> Wisdom is knowing how your short-term actions impact your long-term future.

vision is that it makes decision-making easier. Instead of being distracted by day-to-day decision-making, you can ask this one question: "Is this decision in line with my vision?" That's the main criterion for making the decision. It's like a filter. How much easier does that sound than the back and forth of should I do this or should I not? Your long-term vision becomes your line of accountability for decision-making.

Criteria for Approaching Your Vision

Let's take a look now at our three criteria for approaching your vision.

1. Rethinking your idea of growth
2. Stating your why
3. Rebuilding your foundation as a business owner

1. Rethinking Your Idea of Growth

The problem Anthony faced in building his business was not a lack of initiative, skill, or intelligence. He had all of those, and he was highly successful, at least in the way he understood success. The real problem Anthony faced, as do most advisors, was choosing a limited vision of success. Anthony's vision of success was increased productivity, and because everything follows vision, he achieved that. When he came up against any decision, he asked, "How will this decision impact productivity?" That's a very narrow view. Going back to our running example, it's kind of like asking how each step will affect your foot. If you're focused on the well-being of your foot, how will you notice the markers that show you're on the right path, let alone see what will get you to your destination—the lake?

Having a long-term vision and asking the question, "How will this decision affect my long-term vision?" is how you scale. Because Anthony was unaware of this, his vision capped out at a certain point, and no further productivity was possible. What's more, Anthony's personal and family life suffered greatly during the process. Obviously, Anthony's vision of increasing productivity did not deliver the life or business he really wanted.

What if we were to think of success in different terms? What if there really was more to success than increasing productivity? What if we could define success in terms of freedom rather than only in terms of finances? What would that look like?

Think of it this way. Given the choice, would you rather have a 20 percent increase in production this year or have your business become 20 percent less dependent on you with the same production? Both of those would be a measure of growth, wouldn't they? Both would be great years of growth, just measured in different terms. Most advisors have the mindset that increased production is the only definition of business growth and thus the only definition of success. Yet as we've seen, that way of thinking is not healthy or sustainable. It inevitably leads to burnout.

I often ask advisors how they define growth. Most give some variation of "increased production" or "increased revenue." Then ask them about their stress level. The more successful they are (in their terms), the higher their stress level. Their work consumes them. It doesn't free their time so they can live a better life, one of significance.

I had this conversation with an advisor, Tom, who has one of the most productive businesses in the country, doing more than $50 million a year in new assets. While dining with Tom and his wife, I asked about his stress level. His answer was shocking. "I just want my life back," he said. "I would rather not bring in one more dollar of production and just get my life back. I want to take some of this heavy weight off my shoulders."

Tom's wife put it more starkly. "If he doesn't change something soon, he's going to work himself to death." Does this sound like success to you? It doesn't to me either. It was a hard lesson for him to learn, but it was the most rewarding lesson of his career.

Fast forward twelve months, and Tom went from having twenty-four client meetings a week at burnout to only four per week while doing 70 percent more production per year. The next year he did even better. He was no longer responsible for any of the production or client meetings, yet his business produced more than double pre-burnout levels. And he was taking the majority of his summers off to be with his family. This shift in vision and growth was a turning point, not only in his business but also in his life. In a couple of short years, he built a business to scale.

As you begin to form your vision for your business and your life, make sure it is far-ranging enough to include all the things that matter to you. Increasing production will do you no good in the long run if you don't have the personal bandwidth to sustain it. Increased personal income has no value if you lack the time, energy, and meaningful relationships to enjoy it. And a business that grows more and more dependent on you and your abilities becomes less and less sellable over time.

2. Stating Your Why

Transforming from an advisor to a business owner and ditching the Red Line for the Green Line will not be the most difficult thing you've ever done. I want to assure you that this is doable. You deserve a business that scales, and so does your team. A business that scales allows your team to grow, it empowers their careers, and it helps them meet their professional dreams. For them to align with your vision and be motivated to help you toward it, they need to align with it. Moving from the Red Line to the Green Line can be done.

I've seen many advisors make this switch, and I'm confident you can too. However, it will require a significant change in how you think about and operate your business. There will be some difficult things about it, and you'll need to prepare yourself for that mentally. Every great endeavor begins with a burst of enthusiasm and hopefully finishes with a victory. In the middle, though, it can be difficult. You need to be ready for that, and the best way to prepare is to get clear on why you want to make this change.

Stating your motivation does a couple of things. First, it solidifies your resolve by putting you in touch with your deepest motivation. Many people start off in this business with only a vague idea of why they want to be an advisor. For some, it may sound like a solid career. It may align with their natural abilities, or they may think it's the best way to make a significant income. All of that is fine. But to undertake a major change, you'll need to know what's really driving your choices.

A vision should be much more than just numbers and goals. It should include what you stand for, what's important to you, and the purpose and impact. That is why great visions have a "heart" that captures the heart of others. Personally, my motivation for doing what I do goes far deeper than money or even building a successful business. Growing up, I had a front row seat to the business of financial advising. My father was an advisor, and I was the kid who wanted Daddy's time. He always had to take one more call from a client who needed help, who trusted him to deliver. He didn't want to let them down, and he didn't want to let his family down. I saw the pressure he was under. Fortunately, my dad discovered the secret of scale and was able to see and experience the difference he made, not only in our lives but also in the lives of his clients.

A vision should be much more than just numbers and goals. It should include what you stand for, what's important to you, and the purpose and impact.

From a young age, I felt called to this industry. I felt called to make a difference for advisors. I did this to help others achieve meaningful success in business and gain an amazing quality of life for themselves, their families, and their clients. That's my why. And I firmly believe that guiding elite financial advisors to scale will create a ripple effect of value for anybody who comes in contact with their business. The founder, the team, the clients, and their families will benefit in a positive way. This deep calling will allow me to persevere regardless of the short-term storms I face or obstacles I run into. This calling makes it worth carrying on, and it's why I burned the boats behind me in order to create it. I don't believe money, status, or any other benefit could have given me the drive to take extreme action like a true calling and purpose have. What if this was the case for you and your team? What if you all were aligned on a much deeper way to build a business of significance? This is key to persevering and doing anything great in business and in life.

Before you begin working through Triad's Five Principles to Scale™ for your financial services business, find your driving motivation—your heart or just cause that connects with your highest and best desires. Almost certainly that will involve something more than making money. Your why will touch on the big thing you're hoping to achieve in life, whether that's leaving a legacy, creating more freedom for your own clients, moving others from worry to wealth, or something else that's important to you. Take some time to think it through. Talk about it with your family or closest friends. Write it down, and keep it in a place where you will see it often. This is the fuel that will keep you going through this transition from the Red Line to the Green Line. Without it, you may stumble and drift back to the old road of comfort—the Red Line.

3. Rebuilding Your Foundation as a Business Owner

Creating your vision and discovering your why requires rebuilding your foundation. Going back to our running example, if you're a runner who is used to focusing on each footstep rather than where you want to run that day and how far, then focusing on a bigger goal—where you want to run that day—changes how you approach your run. The same thing happens when you go from being an advisor to being a business owner. Your focus shifts. Suddenly, everything you do within your organization must fit your vision. Anything that doesn't shouldn't have a place in your business.

A business owner's vision is their brand. It's their heart, remember? And everything they do from marketing to sales to managing the client experience aligns with that brand. This alignment always returns to the brand manifesto, which includes core principles, messaging, and more. Every project they do, every initiative they follow aligns with that brand and image.

Most advisors, however, don't have a brand manifesto, which means that every brochure or website overhaul is pieced together as needed but does not fit with their long-term vision of their brand. It's a lot of templated things designed without intention. It's not consistent or congruent with who they are. We believe it's critical to include your brand in your vision so your vision truly impacts everything you do. When you piece things together, you throw too many different things at people, and the more they see, the less they remember.

While this may sound a little overwhelming at first, creating a vision is how you'll stand out. That is how your ideal client will find you. It's how you'll cut through the 6,000 messages consumers in the Attention Economy sift through each day. But it requires work, vision, and rebuilding your foundation.

Rebuilding your foundation means two things:

- Decommoditization
- Systemization

> When you piece things together, you throw too many different things at people and the more you do, the less they remember.

Decommoditizing Your Brand

When a brand is a commodity, it doesn't stand out. There's simply nothing about it that would make a consumer choose it over something else. You probably buy comoditized products. Maybe it's tissue or paper plates or bananas. You don't care which brand is selling them because they all seem the same to you. Most likely, you just buy the cheapest option.

Marketing and branding exist to help ***decommoditize*** brands, or make them stand out. But to decommoditize, you have to have vision. You have to understand what truly sets you apart from other advisors. You have to understand why the person you most want to bring in—your ideal client—would pick you over hundreds of other advisors.

I can tell you right now that it's not the investment returns, fees, or proprietary products—none of these things make you stand out. It's also not your service. Why? Because everyone in this industry provides that. In fact, a recent study[9] shows that when asked "What sets you apart?" more than 70 percent of advisors said, "My service." What sets you apart goes back to your heart,

9 https://www.kitces.com/blog/financial-advisor-great-service-defining-and-differentiating-with-a-cli-ent-ser-%20vice-standard/.

your mission, your vision. Your why is what's different about you, not the portfolio you are offering.

Let me show you what I mean with an example of one of the most recognized brands on the planet—McDonald's.

When McDonald's launched in 1955, it was a standard burger joint. Like the thousands of burger joints you've never heard of, it could have remained "just" a burger joint. However, its owners had vision. They wanted to create a franchise that would stand out from competitors such as Big Boy and become the best burger joint in the country.

But how do you appear "different" when you're selling the exact same thing—in this case, burgers—that everyone else is selling? Just like Big Boy, McDonald's sold a patty with a bun, burger, lettuce, tomato, and pickle.

> To stand out in a sea of sameness, you have to prove that you're more than a commodity and worth paying attention to. You have to decommoditize what you offer.

To stand out in a sea of sameness, you have to prove that you're more than a commodity and worth paying attention to. You have to decommoditize what you offer.

To do this, McDonald's owners did a few things. First, they understood that they were selling a commodity. In the 1960s when McDonald's introduced the Big Mac, the owners understood that just about anyone could grab a burger anywhere in any US city at any time. No one would stop in for a McDonald's burger because they had a tomato, a sesame seed bun, or a pickle on their burger.

They knew they would have to stand out and create something proprietary. Enter the Big Mac. Before McDonald's knew it, people from all over the country were seeking out the Big Mac—two all-beef patties, special sauce, lettuce, cheese, pickles, onions on a sesame seed bun. People loved it! In a sea of sameness, McDonald's stood out. It decommoditized its product and became more than just a burger joint. McDonald's created something proprietary, named it, and trademarked it. McDonald's is the only place you can get a Big Mac.

The awesome thing about McDonald's is that once one proprietary offering was created, it set the stage for others. Now you've got the McFlurry, the McChicken, the McDouble—even the McDelivery—McDonald's version of Uber. Each of these is something consumers seek out. No one asks for ice cream swirled with broken pieces of candy, but they will ask for a McFlurry. It's all about brand.

Are you seeing how this connects to our industry? Do you see how providing legacy planning, great service, investment planning, and more is the same as everyone else? Just like McDonald's, your brand is not about a product. It's about something that's proprietary, something that is unique to you. You have to create the vision to build it. Assuming that you do full retirement planning, based on the CFP boards and like the Big Mac example, you can think of it this way:

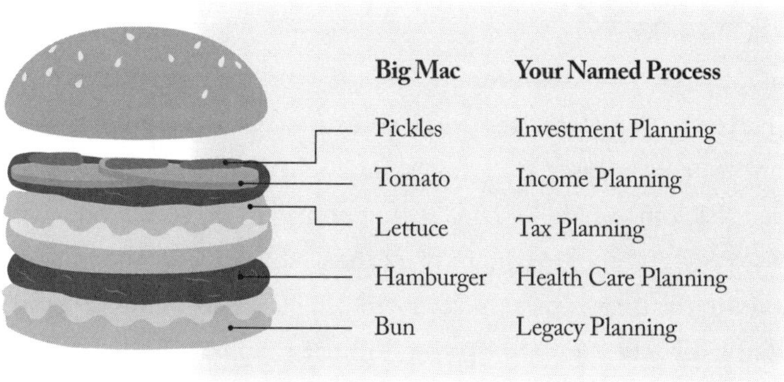

Rather than say you have burger with lettuce, why not name your process, one that covers all five ingredients? Then trademark, it and have a decommoditized brand for what you do.

Over time, you become known for something that is unique and proprietary to you.

Having a product or service that is unique is great, but you have to be able to market it to your audience. Having them at the forefront of your mind at all times is critical. McDonald's knew this too. Instead of hiring a bunch of young women and putting them on roller skates to deliver food to the cars like so many other burger joints, McDonald's decided to target families. Ronald McDonald, the Happy Meal, and the PlayPlace for kids followed. I don't know about your family, but in my family, we end up at McDonald's only when my kids request it. They love it.

Systemizing Your Processes

Decommoditizing your product certainly gets consumers' attention, but it's only sustainable if you can then build systems to support the business you get and the expectations of your customers once they come in for what you do.

One of McDonald's most well-known and brilliant moves was taking Henry Ford's assembly line idea and applying the concept to a burger joint. Before creating this process, most burger joints ran their businesses like this: someone took a customer's order, went back to the kitchen, made the food, delivered the food to the customer, and took payment from the customer. Can you imagine waiting for that to happen after ordering a burger? Painful, right? That led McDonald's to make a brilliant change.

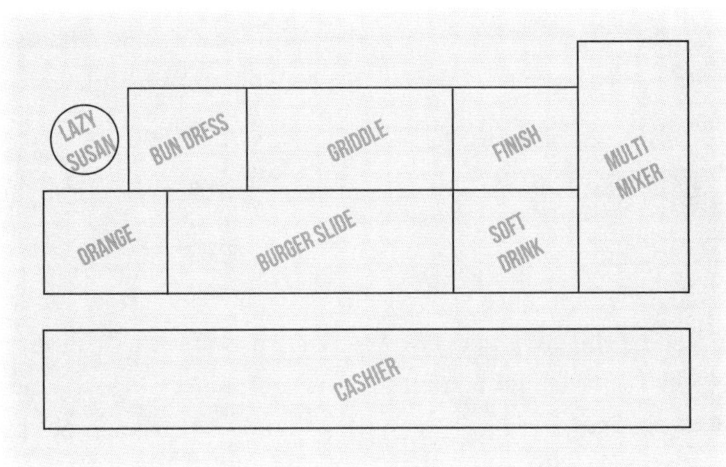

McDonald's introduced the Speedee Service System, a twelve-person line where each person had one job to do. Someone took orders. Another person flipped burgers, and yet another added condiments. This completely changed the way things were done, making McDonald's faster and more consistent than other franchises. As a result, burger production increased to twenty burgers an hour. Creating this system was incredible for the customer's experience and also benefited business volume.

To further systemize, McDonald's also did this:

- Limited its menu to nine items. It was previously expansive and often varied by region.
- Eliminated all silverware and glassware (no washing or storing).
- Opted for handheld food items (faster table turnaround, and consumers could eat while driving).

These simple, clear processes and offerings were easily replicated throughout the country. Consumers knew what to expect from McDonald's wherever they were. It allowed McDonald's to scale on a national level. By giving each person a clear role so they could specialize in what they do, McDonald's increased the quality of its products. It moved from a jack-of-all-trades model to a specialist model. Finally, McDonald's systems were so simple that today, a sixteen-year-old can run the business. That's how dialed in the process became.

There's no way McDonald's could have done this if the owners hadn't had a clear vision of what they wanted to become. If they didn't know where they wanted to go or what they wanted to do as a franchise, they never would have invented the Big Mac or systemized their processes. It would have been much easier to just have just kept doing things normally rather than inventing a new way of doing things. But their vision was bigger than a small burger joint, which led to incredible innovation to improve.

Chapter 6
Transformational Takeaways

- Without an exciting vision, you won't have an exciting business.
- Vision should be a long-term view of where you want to end up.
- Approaching vision requires:
    - Rethinking your idea of growth
    - Stating your why
    - Rebuilding your foundation as a business owner
- Rebuilding your foundation means:
    - Decommoditization, or using your vision to stand out from other financial advisors
    - Systemization, or putting the proper processes in place that will allow your business to optimize and scale

7

HOW TO CREATE YOUR VISION

I made the transition from the Red Line to the Green Line out of desperation. I had no other choice. I had to change. But my biggest fear throughout the process was that I would take too hard of a corrective turn in the process and wreck my business as an end result. So I knew I needed to take one step back in order to take two steps forward.

— Top advisor

Chapter 7 Transformational Targets

- Prepare to adjust your vision over time.
- Your vision should be exciting, inclusive, and set for the longrun.
- Your vision will bring you to scale.

Creating vision is more art than science. It involves sorting the many threads of your own aspirations and your customers' needs and then assembling them into a clear, specific picture that will guide you into the future. So how do you do that?

Like many advisors, I'm an eager, ambitious guy. When I get a good idea, I run with it. Knowing that about myself, I knew I had to do something to ensure that the business I created—Triad Partners—would be something I would be proud of and would want to keep for the long term. Without intention and a clear vision to hold me accountable, I knew I'd be at risk of following the pattern I'd watched with many advisors who made a big change in their business. After a year or two, they'd become bored with it. Sure, they were successful in growing the business, but they still weren't satisfied. Before long, they jumped on the next big idea—a new marketing campaign or sales strategy—and started all over. I wanted none of that. I knew that whatever I would do next had to be intentional. I didn't want to wake up five years later and realize I'd created something I no longer wanted. I needed a clear destination, right from the very start.

For me, the Bible has been a great source of wisdom. One of my favorite verses is Psalm 46:10, "Be still, and know that I am God." As I recalled that and the many other passages that speak of the importance of taking time for quiet reflection, I knew that was exactly what I needed. I tend to be a hard charger, pursuing my mission full speed ahead. So before I started my next chapter of building Triad Partners, I wanted to take some time to simply be still. I ended up taking six weeks off as a kind of sabbatical. I wanted to hit the reset button and do a lot of thinking.

During that time, I did more than think about what I wanted.

I reflected on all the things other advisors had told me over the years. I replayed conversations with advisors, friends, and mentors. Many of them had told me what was missing from their businesses or their lives, their frustration points and problems, and their aspirations. I listened to them and reflected on their thoughts. Before building what is now Triad, I wanted to be sure that what I built deserved to exist because it served the advisors I love working with, solved their problems, and made a difference in their lives.

One advisor voiced a common theme. He told me, "I miss the good old days when our peer group was smaller." Others said, "The bigger the FMO business has gotten, I feel it's more like a vendor and less like a partnership." Several mentioned feeling distant from these relationships, that they were much more transactional. Others said they felt like just a number, not a true mentee when interacting with their business coaches or vendors.

I'll never forget a call I received years ago from an amazing advisor and friend I had worked with for more than a decade. He said, "Shawn, this industry is failing me." He had increased his business tenfold but wanted me to know that the industry was falling short. He had stopped going to industry conferences where there were hundreds of people in the crowd and one "hero" on stage. He stopped using the templates offered by the industry because they felt like "shiny objects" that were really more of a distraction than anything else. He was convinced that the templates hurt his brand. He said, "I want and need a true partner who will help me learn to scale. I don't need a product vendor."

That conversation made a big impact on my destiny and purpose and changed the trajectory of my career. I chose to not ignore it but to listen carefully, understand it, and then later build a business to change it.

During this time of reflection, I remembered my own experience and how it changed over the years. I remembered the early days when I had a small group of advisors who truly knew each other and cared for each other. I remembered the sense of community and connection, the unity of us all running together to build a business that we loved. Then, as time wore on, I found myself in a place where I had to rent a restaurant that seated 500 people in order to host a dinner that had been much more intimate years ago. I felt like a politician as I ran around saying hello to my advisors. I learned to enter and exit conversations in two to three minutes, just so I could say hi to as many people as possible over a few hours. That sucked my energy, and it wasn't fun for me, the advisors, or my wife who was with me but had to sit by herself at the dinner table.

As I processed this, I knew the things my advisors and I had experienced had to inform my vision. I knew that if my vision included their view—what they wanted and needed—and what I wanted in my own life, we would have a business that deserved to exist. Knowing what the advisors longed for in their businesses and in their lives was a huge advantage to Triad in order to create the right vision for our future from day one. Ironically, what the advisors wanted and what I wanted were the same—a sense of purpose, connection, and joy—a life of significance. They didn't want a product vendor to do business with. They didn't want to feel like a number at big industry events or reactive service standards. They preferred a small group of peers with similar values who cared for each other and did business and life together. They wanted the challenge and guidance that a true partner would provide in order to build a business of significance rather than solely seeking monetary gain or material things.

> Ironically, what the advisors wanted and what I wanted were the same—a sense of purpose, connection, and joy—a life of significance.

The advisors wanted to know they were doing meaningful work—work they loved—that genuinely impacted the lives of people they helped. That's exactly what I wanted too.

This was not a step-by-step process. My vision did not appear in a single burst of inspiration. It involved time, listening, thinking, chatting with people I loved and trusted, and reading. By the end of my six-week sabbatical, I had arrived at a point of perfect clarity. As I closed out that period, a single thought crystallized in my mind. "I want to create a business I never want to retire from."

I knew what it was like to have a sense of excitement about my work that comes from having purpose and seeing real progress. And I knew what it was like to work in a business that offered neither of those things. I knew that if I had a business I loved, enjoyed, and was excited to work for, it would not feel like work at all. It would enhance my life, and I'd never want to stop doing it. I also knew that a business like that would not only bless my life but would also bring joy and satisfaction to many others. Having that clear vision, I was confident I could reverse-engineer the process in order to create it.

The Advisor Transformation provides the fundamental principles you need to create a business that scales. It's a blueprint for Green Line growth. Having read this far, you must be committed to creating that kind of business, one that will give you unlimited growth, freedom, and joy—**#DBDL**. But before you start building, I urge you to take time to envision what success looks like to you because you can create any business you can envision. Remember, your vision is the engine. It will power your business in whatever direction you choose. Scale is the destination.

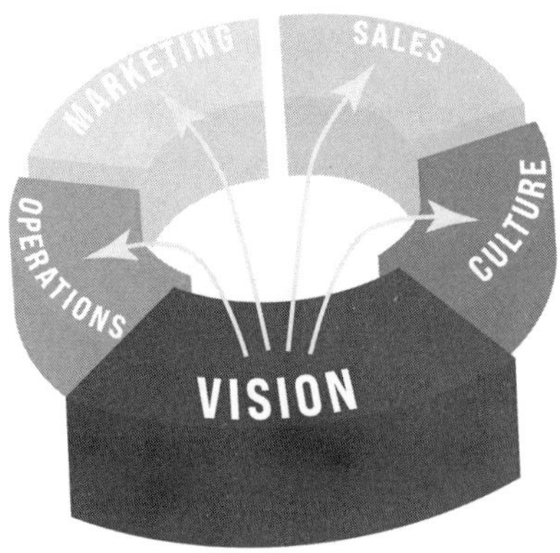

When Triad onboards new advisors, we ask them to envision the next three years for marketing, sales, culture, and operations. What is their ideal future? What do they want from their business? How many teammates do they have? What's the culture like? What does their brand convey? What do they want from their life? We also ask them to create "champagne moments" or wins along the way that are worth popping a bottle of bubbly for. This is a great way to get them thinking about vision.

In the end, your business will be as unique as you and your vision. However, I've discovered a few common themes that leaders in our industry consider when creating their vision.

1. Unlimited growth
2. Freedom
3. Joy
4. Sellability
5. Impact
6. Shareability
7. Clarity

Unlimited Growth

Entrepreneurs are wired for growth. Progress means happiness. No entrepreneur wants to build a business to a certain point and then coast. Your vision must anticipate and expect unlimited growth.

Freedom

Most advisors are willing to work hard, especially at the beginning. That's how they get stuck on the Red Line. More work produces more results, so it feels like progress, but it's not. Yet all advisors want to reach a place of freedom. They want a business that delivers more freedom, not less, over time. Your vision can help set up a future of freedom that does not force you to give up on your growth.

Joy

For the vast majority of people, success at work and happiness are linked in some way. We feel good when we're thriving. We all want to wake up in the morning excited about the day ahead. The quickest way to create joy is to have an exciting vision for the future that people want to wake up to each day and be part of.

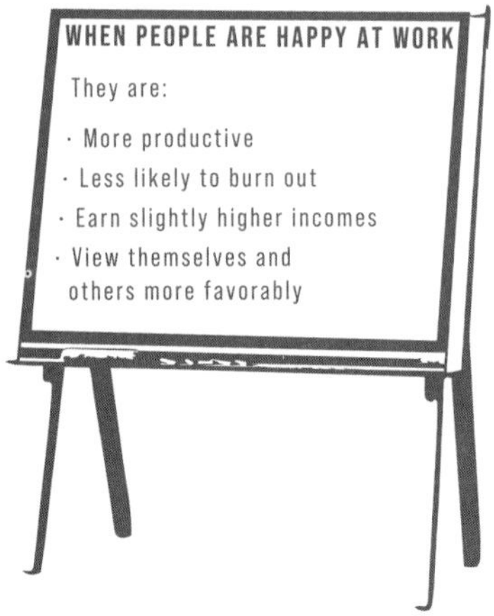

Sellability

Every business owner receives compensation in two ways. The first is the income generated by the company's profits. That's where most business owners, especially Red Line advisors who are not yet thinking like business owners, focus their attention. The second is through the equity gained in the value of the business over time. Most advisors envision a day when they will no longer operate their practice. They'll either retire or perhaps simply sell the business and begin a new venture. Either way, they want to build something that has value in its own right and can be sold at some point. Whether your exit strategy is to one day sell the business or not, you should create a business that has value. Fortunately, building a business that maximizes growth, freedom, and joy also improves the equity value of your business. So consider sellability while working through your vision.

Impact

Regardless of whether you plan to sell your business someday or not, create one that impacts the lives of those around you. Rather than selling widgets and having transactional relationships, make a difference. A business of significance creates real relationships with appreciative clients who genuinely love what you do and the difference you make. In the long term, this is a much more fulfilling and motivating factor than money.

Shareability

Think, create, and share your vision for the future. This is critical for creating a truly scalable company. You, your team, your family, your clients—all of them need to know what your vision is for the company. It gives them buy-in and also helps you remain accountable to that vision.

Clarity

A vision is a mental picture of a future reality, so it must be clear and specific. Having that vision in mind gives you a specific destination and direction. It enables you to make the right decisions. In short, it propels you toward your goal. In order to do that, it has to be clear enough and detailed enough to help you make day-to-day decisions. Then you can reverse-engineer the steps that will get you there.

Your vision is not a step-by-step plan for building your business. In fact, I advise against creating a detailed project plan that lays out each step of the process along with a deadline. Project plans have their place, but the process of building a scalable business has too many variables to fit neatly into a spreadsheet. And you don't know enough yet to list all the steps that will be required. Remember, you're running to the lake, not thinking about your shoes and rocks and feet—not at this stage.

Instead, a clear, specific vision helps you answer this question: "What's next?" It helps you determine the next one, two, or three things you need to do, and it ensures that they're aligned with your desired outcome. In order to make decisions today, you have to know where you want to end up in the long term. In order to have vision, you have to know the destination you are after with complete clarity.

Having a vision keeps you walking with your head up and eyes forward. Once you've hammered out your vision, write it down, and keep it visible to yourself and others. The worst thing you can do with your vision is to put it in a binder and tuck it in a drawer. If your vision is not written down and reviewed often, it will quickly disappear.

While your vision will exist on paper, it's much more than that. If you stick to it, it will become a part of your company's DNA. Your mission—the one on paper—is the path to a future that aligns you and everyone you work with. Your mission is to bring it to life. So:

- Be sure your vision excites you about the future.
- Share that exciting vision with your team.
- Build and rally around your vision like never before.

Be Sure Your Vision Excites You About the Future

Your vision has to be exciting. This is what I labored over during my sabbatical. I knew that if my vision for the company didn't connect with my deepest motivations and if it didn't excite me, it would not be sustainable. If your vision doesn't excite you, how could it possibly excite anyone else? A great vision grabs you by the heart and says, "Follow me!"

An exciting vision will make everything in your business easier. It will bleed into all areas of your business. It's like a tailwind,

> A great vision grabs you by the heart and says, "Follow me!"

providing momentum, consistency, and clarity for every step of your journey. If it's strong, exciting, and inspirational, your teammates will wake up every day, excited to be part of it. You will attract incredible talent—people who want to latch on to your vision. Everything in your work life will be easier if you have an exciting vision.

Your Vision Litmus Test:

Curious if your vision is exciting?
Answer these questions:

Are my company's best years before me or behind me?

How would my team answer that question?

If you (and they) answer "before me," you're moving toward vision, a bright future that will excite both you and your team.

When I started Triad Partners, I learned very early that I had to sell my team on our vision, just like I would sell a client on the firm. Quite simply, my vision was to help advisors create unlimited growth and freedom in their business and life. From my perspective, the sales process is simply transferring a belief I have to others. That's what makes it easy for me to sell our company and our vision. I really believe in it. Because of that, I've been able to gather an incredible team of high achievers who are equally excited by our vision. In fact, multiple team members picked up and moved their families across the country to join us. Many took significant pay cuts in order to work for our startup. That's the power of an exciting vision. If our vision was boring, routine, nonexistent, or unintentional, that never would have happened.

Years ago, I attended a small group with other entrepreneurs in Silicon Valley. One of the speakers had recently sold his company for nearly $1 billion. He had created a "unicorn" in the tech industry that had explosive growth in a very short time. He grew it to hundreds of team members and attracted many of the best tech talent. Many of them left large, stable, well-known tech companies to join him. One of the conference attendees asked the question the majority of us wanted to know. "What's the key to getting great team members and keeping them?"

#DBDL

His answer was simple. "What I found was more than benefits, pay, and other things is—great people want to be a part of an exciting company that is doing big things. Our vision and growth kept attracting the best in the industry and kept the ones who were with us excited about what we were building."

The excitement those team members had each day meant more than the stability or comfort of working with a big, well-established company name. And here's the bottom line. If this company had a small vision, would it have attracted great talent? Big thinkers attract great talent. Small thinkers with an unexciting vision attract people who are "looking for a job."

So if your vision is big and exciting, you will find great people and get a much higher level of commitment from them than if your vision is small or uninspiring. This also creates incredible alignment so everybody is moving toward the same goal. Alignment is something you can't fake, and it's one of the most important things for your business and your team. If they are all moving in the same direction, you'll get much more done than you ever thought possible.

You need a vision that represents an exciting future, and you need to share it with your team over and over. An exciting vision creates an exciting business. Nobody wants a "job" that's simply doing the same things every day in exchange for a paycheck. People want to be part of something meaningful and exciting. A powerful vision provides that.

Nobody wants a "job" that's simply doing the same things every day in exchange for a paycheck. People want to be part of something meaningful and exciting. A powerful vision provides that.

We identify where they are today and what they want for the future, and we do deep work together to go down the path of creating it. Often, team members share that they've never really talked about this as a group or been included in a conversation about what to build. Telling a team your vision won't get the buy-in from them that you'll get when they're part of building that vision.

Usually this process reveals a lot, including the culture your team wants and the gaps that maybe the founder doesn't see. I'll usually ask, "How many of you want to be part of a company that does exciting things? A company that really grows and is special?"

Every time, they all raise their hands.

I've realized something really cool through this process. Team members often have differences, but they have a common mission. Rather than focusing on the differences, we focus on the common thing, which is way more important. Before long, their differences become an advantage. Their different experiences, perspectives, and personalities allow them to complement each other more than if they were all the same. When everybody realizes they want the

When everybody realizes they want the same thing and need to work together to create it, it's amazing how they step up and willingly play the role the company needs them to play because they know their role matters.

same thing and need to work together to create it, it's amazing how they step up and willingly play the role the company needs them to play because they know their role matters.

Sure, in this business, sometimes the main sales person gets a lot of the glory. But each role is needed, each role matters, and everybody on the team has to choose what the team needs more than what their own individual needs are. As NCAA basketball coach Bill Self said, "It's not the greatest players that win the championship. It's the players that play the best together." It's team approach. The more we realize that, the better chance we have to build what we all want.

Share that Exciting Vision with Your Team

I've been talking about my vision and your vision. But I don't believe a compelling vision is ever the product of a single individual. Great visions are created by a collection of people. That's part of what gives visions such power—they are seen by many people. That's why I spent so much time thinking about my clients when crafting the vision for Triad. By listening to them and understanding the problems and challenges they faced, I was able to craft a vision that would fit not just me but thousands of others. I was really distilling our common vision. As I mentioned, I wanted to help advisors create unlimited growth and freedom in their business and life. Even writing those words still makes me excited about the opportunity to do this work.

So in one sense, the critical question in creating vision is not "What do I want to build?" but:

- What do my customers want from this company?
- What are their needs and desires?
- What can I offer that will make a difference in their lives?
- What will make them excited about working with me?

The place where your passion and your clients' needs align is the starting point for a powerful and exciting vision.

Everyone uses different methods to create their own vision. I recommend using a process similar to the one I used when I started Triad Partners. Take a vision retreat or sabbatical, time away from your business, to think about what you really want to build. I had the ability to take six weeks, but your process doesn't need to be that long. I have a client who literally went into the mountains for three days to get peace and quiet, and to think. The point is, get some space that will allow you to think freely. That's nearly impossible to do amid the frantic pace of daily life. You need time and space to sort out the various thoughts in your mind and form a clear, specific vision for the future about what excites you so you can put it on paper, remember it, and share it.

Build and Rally around Your Vision Like Never Before

The vision you're creating today will not be your last-ever vision. As you pursue building your amazing vision, you will gain more insight and information. For you to not use that to your advantage would be foolish. Your vision will constantly improve, and you need to be flexible. You're creating the core now, but you will continue polishing it or buffing the edges as you build. This is not only okay, it's highly beneficial. Your vision is not a one-and-done thing. Your vision is a target, and it's okay if that target moves over time. Life cannot be set in stone. When revisiting your vision is ongoing, it becomes part of you and the way you see the future.

Visions are not stagnant, and they are not a single piece of paper you tack on the wall. One of the visions we helped an advisor create was thirty-three pages. It could be a small book. When you don't think about the details of your vision, you will run into problems.

Your vision is your guide. The more complete it is, the greater your probability of success in the long term.

Once you arrive at your vision, you'll need to sell it over and over again. Any vision worth pursuing cannot be achieved alone. You must enlist a team around your vision and transfer the belief to them. Talk about it with your team frequently. Once every month is not too often. Keep them inspired by what you are building together. Tell your clients about it. Let them buy in to more than the products you offer. Help them get excited about the future you are building. They're part of it too.

#DBDL

Finally, remember that you will not achieve your vision by dabbling—just like you won't achieve scale by dabbling. To be effective, a vision must inspire your full commitment over a very long time. It will certainly demand your best effort. Commit to your vision, and bring others into it. Over time, it will become the way you do business—and life. And all of those involved in it will believe in it just like you do and help carry the weight.

You can do this! A vision without commitment is powerless. A vision backed by commitment is an unstoppable force. Commit to bringing your vision to life.

CHAPTER 7
TRANSFORMATIONAL TAKEAWAYS

- Your vision does not need to appear in a single burst of inspiration. It can—and should—evolve over time.
- Things to consider whencreating your vision:
  - Unlimited growth
  - Joy
  - Sellability
  - Impact
  - Shareability
  - Clarity
- Having a strong vision is the first step to scale.
- The three keys to bringing your vision to life include:
  - Be sure your vision excites you about the future
  - Share that exciting vision with your team
  - Build and rally around it like never before
- You cannot dabble in your vision. You must go all in.

Looking to set your vision for scale? Check out additional resources here.

SECTION 4

OPERATIONS

So you've got a great vision and know what's been working so far with sales and marketing (more on that later). But in order to grow, the operations side of your business has to be ready to scale. And there's not a single advisor out there who has scaled their business by marketing or selling alone. Not a single one.

Your operations need to be set up in such a way that your time and each team member's time is optimized based on each person's specific skills and the value they bring to the company. That means:

1. Working well as a team
2. Giving up control so each person can play the role the company needs them to play

I know. Giving up control is a tough one for many people who are used to doing everything on their own. But the more you try to control your business, the more your business will actually control you. You have to work with your team, delegate like a pro, and understand how your approach to delegating—and your infrastructure—will change over time.

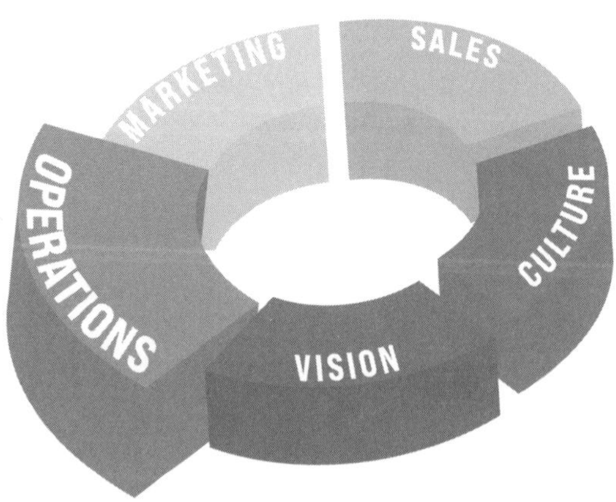

But before you can delegate, you have to know where you're going and why. That is why you've already crushed the vision section of *The Advisor Transformation*. Right? When you have clarity, you can clearly guide your team members as they move through their careers within your organization.

In Section 4, we will talk about:

- The time/value equation
- Where your time is really spent
- The average value of an hour of your time over a year
- The value of an hour of your time based on your current role and responsibilities

Are you ready for your next step toward unlimited growth, freedom, and joy?

8

OPTIMIZE YOUR TIME

Learning how to properly delegate was the key to freeing me for the transformation.

— Top advisor

Chapter 8 Transformational Targets

- Familiarize yourself with the four principles of time and use those principles to determine where you spend your time.
- Understand that your highest value tasks will shift as your business grows.
- Check each teammate's productivity and enjoyment against Michael Hyatt's Freedom Compass.

Riding the Red Line of Success is not a matter of activity, energy, or chance. It's a very calculated relationship with time, and each minute is a priceless, finite commodity that's deployed with laser-focused intention. To create a business that scales, you need to be very intentional about where your time and energy are spent. That starts with a deep understanding of the value of your time as it relates to your business.

If you master the relationship between your time and the growth of your business, your business will scale. If you don't, you'll continue on the Red Line, sinking more and more hours into your business until you are exhausted. Optimizing your time is one of the most important skills you must learn in order to scale because you cannot have infinite growth if your business is dependent on a finite resource—your time or your team members' time.

Optimizing your time is one of the most important skills you must learn in order to scale because you cannot have infinite growth if your business is dependent on a finite resource—your time or your team members' time.

It's critically important that you have a good understanding of what you and your team spend time on and what return you're getting for that investment. That allows you to prioritize your focus—and theirs—as your company grows.

These priorities will be a moving target over time, but the better you understand how to leverage time, the more opportunity you'll have to optimize your productivity. That leads to greater and greater growth in productivity.

Let's walk through four things that will help you truly understand the value of your own time. Then we'll see how to make better use of your time. Here's how to make better use of your time.

1. Understand time and value are a simple equation
2. Identify where your time is really being spent
3. Know the average value of an hour of your time in a year
4. Understand the value of an hour of your time based on your current role and responsibilities

1. Understand time and value are a simple equation

Years ago, I spoke before a group of advisors in Ohio. I knew that one of the advisors, Mike, was a mega producer and very well-known in the industry. During my time with these advisors, I spoke about the principles of scaling a business, much like you are reading in *The Advisor Transformation*. When I finished, Mike approached me and asked if we could talk. I agreed, and we strolled outside and started chatting. He shared that he was making more money than he had ever dreamed of but was at the end of his rope. By now, stories like Mike's were very familiar to me. He'd been working sixty to seventy hours a week, had three kids at home, including a newborn, and was simply out of time. He had nothing left to give to the business or his family. He was ready to cry uncle.

"I just don't have enough time," he said.

I wanted to dial in a little more on his pain points because it's impossible to help anyone with this problem without understanding the source of it. I asked, "Of those sixty hours a week that you're working, how many appointments do you have with clients?"

"On average? Seven to ten."

"Great! How many of those are new clients, and how many are existing clients?"

"Probably 70 percent are existing clients."

"How long are the appointments?"

"An hour, but I spend half an hour preparing."

"Okay, so on the high end you spend about fifteen hours per week doing what you do best—meeting with clients and preparing for those meetings. Is that right?" I could see the lights go on.

"Yes, that sounds about right," he said.

"So where do the other forty-five hours go each week?" I asked.

"Well, I do a lot of things," he said. "I spend time doing random service work, following up with financial companies, answering emails, managing staff—I'm actually not that sure, to be honest. But it's non stop clutter in my day. I feel like I have to do all these little things or the results may be lower quality than what my clients are used to."

Sound familiar?

Mike was facing the crisis moment everyone faces on the Red Line. Will I burn myself out in the business? Or will I let it plateau so I can get my life back? I let Mike know that rather than crying uncle, he needed to understand where his time was really being spent so he could leverage it to his advantage. It's nearly impossible to fix a problem you don't see and understand. It's also impossible for a coach to help anyone who doesn't know where they're spending their time. So I asked Mike if we could go through how he spent his time so I could get a better understanding of his situation in hopes of finding a solution. He agreed.

2. Identify where your time is really being spent

Like Mike, entrepreneurs often want a quick fix and clear direction in order to pull themselves out of the problem of not having enough time. Unfortunately, a quick, simple fix often leads to more problems. You can't fix a problem you can't see. So before pointing someone down a path to solve a problem, you first have to fully understand where their time really goes. In order to understand exactly how to solve Mike's problem, we had to run an exercise that would uncover the truth about his time. Mike was quite surprised by the results.

When Mike and I met the following week, I asked him to write down everything he did during his workdays for one week, starting with Monday and ending with Friday, from 8:00 a.m. until he was done each day. "List everything you do," I said, "including answering the phone, calling a financial institution, meeting with a client—any and all tasks, no matter what they are. Every detail matters." The next week when Mike and I got together, I asked him for the results. He said, "I'm sorry, I didn't have time to do that."

At that point, we really had to have a heart to heart. I didn't want to waste my time or his time despite the irony that he let the day to day take priority over finding a potential solution to his problem. I asked Mike for permission to empower one of his team members to help. I gave his administrative assistant instructions to mirror Mike for a week and write down everything he did. A week later, we did a three-way Zoom call and discussed the results.

We went line by line to identify where he was spending his time. It was simple enough to get the totals for each category. Now we had a baseline for how he was spending his time.

You can try this exercise yourself. Just log your time in fifteen-minute increments throughout the day. If you'd like the same worksheet, check out our resources page.

3. Know the average value of an hour of your time in a year

Every task you undertake has value whether it's interacting with clients, managing emails, or liaising with financial institutions. However, this doesn't mean you should evenly distribute your time among them.

After analyzing Mike's time distribution, we evaluated the worth of his time across different tasks.

First, we established the average value of an hour of Mike's work. We did that by dividing his annual revenue by the estimated hours he works per year. The results were revealing—Mike generated roughly $2 million per year. Using the standard forty-hour work week and assuming he worked fifty weeks per year (a total of 2,000 hours), Mike's hourly rate came out to be about $1,000. This revelation left him stunned.

"Is my hourly rate truly worth that much?"

Visualizing how much he potentially spent on emails and calls in a single day at that rate was a reality check, as it is for many in our industry.

You can determine your time's worth similarly. Divide your annual earnings by 2,000 hours. The outcome might surprise you since many aren't aware of their time's genuine worth. If they were, perhaps they wouldn't squander it so recklessly. Despite all time being valuable, its worth isn't uniform.

4. Understand the value of an hour of your time based on your current role and responsibilities

Yes, Mike's average hourly value stood at $1,000, but that represented an average across varying tasks over the year. Some tasks were more productive than others. But on average, Mike proved to be an invaluable asset to his organization.

We did a breakdown based on his hourly rate:

Task	Value
3 client meetings	$3,000
1 hour staff meetings	$1,000
1 hour calling vendors	$2,000
2 hours answering email	$2,000
Total	**$8,000**

Using Mike's time distribution, I set out to determine if his schedule was truly optimized. Here's one question I posed:

"Mike, would you pay someone $1,000 an hour for this task?" Not surprisingly, the majority of Mike's tasks didn't justify such a rate. An interesting observation is that many professionals often perceive themselves to be busier than they actually are. Distractions throughout the day may give an illusion of productivity, but the true cost is a lack of focus and wasted time.

Diving deeper, I noticed that some tasks on Mike's calendar were significantly more valuable than the $1,000 per hour average. For instance, our analysis showed that the average sales meeting on his schedule was valued between $3,000 and $5,000 per hour.

Engaging with potential clients was Mike's top priority. Surprisingly, he only had twelve of those meetings per month, averaging three a week. Here's how the math broke down.

First appointments	12 hours
Second appointments	9 hours
Third appointments	6 hours
Total per month	27 hours
Total per year	**324 hours**

The eye-opener? Roughly $1 million of Mike's annual revenue came from new clients. That translated to an astounding $3,086 per hour, revealing a missed opportunity. Mike was dedicating merely twenty-seven hours each month to his most valuable activity.

Mike had been vastly successful while leveraging just a fifth of his total available time. The secret to increased revenue and reduced working hours was clear—more client meetings and fewer lower-value tasks.

While sales meetings typically translate to higher revenues, our analyses with marketing initiatives sometimes show even more impressive returns. With Mike, his primary client acquisition strategy was through speaking engagements. These events, although fruitful, required significant prep time, with tasks of varying value.

Our objective became clear—identify the exact worth of each hour Mike worked. By assigning a value to each task, we could optimize Mike's productivity. Here were the subsequent steps:

1. Define the value of each of Mike's tasks
2. Direct his focus solely toward high-value tasks

How to Leverage Your Time by Focusing on High-Value Tasks

As I analyzed Mike's daily tasks, I noticed several areas where he was investing his $1,000 per hour on tasks that clearly didn't match that value. Routine tasks such as sitting on hold with financial companies, responding to emails, and doing general office administration were consuming his valuable time.

Mike's expertise meant that he should be concentrating on tasks that maximize office productivity. Often, the founding advisor's time is the first potential area of optimization.

We found that Mike was spending the majority of his time doing things he shouldn't be doing. He had a very capable team who could easily take those tasks off his plate, and that would optimize the output of the whole team collectively.

Mike began to see the problem, but he still had a few concerns.

He felt he couldn't trust someone else to do some of the tasks he was used to doing and still keep up the level of quality his clients expected. That's a typical fear, one we'll talk about more in the following chapters. But rather than confront that fear directly, I decided to try a little exercise with Mike. The next time we talked, I said, "Hey, I've got good news for you, man. I have a friend, Holly, who works for an advisor near you. She already does 90 percent of the work on your task list that we need to remove."

"Oh?" Mike said.

"Yeah," I continued. "I just talked to her yesterday, and, oddly enough, she's open to a new opportunity. You could hire her right now and instantly offload the majority of these tasks. That'd save you a ton of time each week, which you can then reallocate to higher-value things like we discussed."

Mike was in disbelief. "Really? I'd love to hire her. How much does she make?"

I pulled out a piece of paper, wrote down Holly's requested salary, folded it, and then slid it across the table.

Mike eagerly picked it up, opened it, and read it. His eyes popped, and his jaw dropped. "Shawn, are you crazy? A thousand dollars an hour for Holly?"

I said, "Mike, you've already hired Holly for $1,000 per hour. Holly is you. Every time you call a financial institution, screen your own emails, or take the quick administrative request, you are costing your company over $1,000 per hour."

Most advisors run their business the way Mike did by stepping over dollars to pick up pennies. If you've determined that your time is worth $1,000 per hour, by doing $25 per hour work, you actually cost your business $975 per hour doing that $25 per hour task. If you agree that it would be foolish to hire Holly for $1,000 an hour to complete these tasks, you're right. And you need to fire yourself from that work immediately.

When I pointed that out to Mike, he thought about it for a second and then said, "I can't believe how much I have been handicapping my own success by not letting go and letting someone else do those tasks."

The worst part of this was that Mike had a very capable team. The problem wasn't them or their ability to own these tasks. It was Mike's willingness to give up control. Once Mike started the transition, there were multiple occasions where his team members said, "I've been telling you for years that I'd prefer to handle that for you."

The time/value equation was exactly what Mike needed to see in order to realize how much he was costing his business by not letting go and allowing his team to help him optimize his time.

He knew his team would need proper training, and he knew he'd have to get uncomfortable and allow them to take things off his plate. But in the end, it would be one of the best things he could do for his business. He was committed to doing it, one step at a time.

As this started to free Mike up, his team was more empowered, and Mike was able to reallocate his time to do the things his business wanted him to do in order for it to grow. As a bonus, Mike's enjoyment of the business increased as well. It turned out that he didn't actually like most of the tasks he'd been holding onto. The high-value tasks—meeting with clients and prospective clients—were the things he really enjoyed. Yet he had been spending the minority of his time doing them.

Time: An Ever-Fluctuating Asset

In essence, while all tasks have value, their worth differs. The key is to invest your time in tasks that offer the highest returns. Grasping this time/value equation allows you to focus on your most productive activities as you identify and eliminate time drains. I'll delve into this optimal use of time in the next chapter.

It's crucial to note that the Time–Value Principle is universally applicable, not just for business owners. Typically, we introduce this concept starting with the company's founder. Yet it's beneficial for the entire team to undergo this exercise. Often we discover that bottlenecks hindering a company's growth are not just the owner but one or two pivotal team members.

A recent coaching call with a business team highlighted this issue. The business owner felt he had a balanced workload and stated, "Life's good on my end." However, his long-standing team member, deeply loyal and dedicated for almost ten years, expressed her overwhelming workload and impending burnout. This disparity in perspective was an eye-opener.

Further discussions revealed that this wasn't an isolated issue. While the owner had efficiently delegated tasks, it inadvertently created bottlenecks among a few team members. This had to be addressed to ensure sustainable business growth.

Our solution? We applied the Time–Value Principle. By evaluating where each member's time was invested and categorizing tasks based on their value and relevance to individual expertise, we found that seasoned professionals were bogged down with basic administrative tasks. Think about the potential impact if a strategic hire could free up twenty hours of a skilled team member's week. Often, the solution isn't necessarily new hires but rather a reorganization and effective delegation. Overcoming delegation hesitancy, a challenge faced by many, is crucial for time optimization.

Consider applying this evaluation across your team. You'll likely find a common pattern—many are stretched thin, attempting to handle everything instead of smartly allocating their time. As you protect and prioritize the high-level activities, versus being eaten alive by the low-level activities you will gradually lift the whole team's ability to grow professionally and in the roles and responsibilities they have.

As you protect and prioritize the high-level activities versus being eaten alive by the low-leverage activities you will gradually lift the whole team's ability to grow professionally and in the roles and responsibilities they have.

As your business evolves, the allocation of time and tasks for you and your team will inevitably change. This is a fluid process. Rapid business growth translates to frequent role shifts. Revisiting the Time–Value Principle is therefore essential. As roles evolve, the best use of your time today might not align with the demands in a few years. Periodically assessing the value of time for you and your team is pivotal for sustained productivity. Empowering well-trained individuals to focus on their strengths enhances their overall contributions as well as fulfillment.

Growth often hinges on discerning what tasks to undertake and which to decline. By deliberately rejecting low-leverage tasks, you pave the way for more meaningful contributions. Reflect on the worth of your time. Which activities yield the most value? Which tasks should you relinquish so you can dedicate more time to high-value endeavors? Addressing these questions sets you on the path to scaling successfully.

The Freedom Compass

Now that we've zoned in on how to maximize team members' productivity, there's a second exercise to take this even further. In terms of productivity, focusing on your high-value tasks is really important to scale. But over time, you will also want to make sure you are passionate and doing the work you are most suited for. The same goes for your team. When you have people doing things they aren't well suited for or don't enjoy, it won't work in the long term.

The Freedom Compass is a great way to solve this. It was created by well-known business leader and author Michael Hyatt to show where maximum productivity happens. As you can see, productivity is maximized in the Desire Zone, the midpoint between a person's passion and proficiency.

If you take someone on your team who is really into data and loves living in the weeds and ask them to be a service advisor, they will fall short both in passion and proficiency. In effect, that

The Freedom Compass

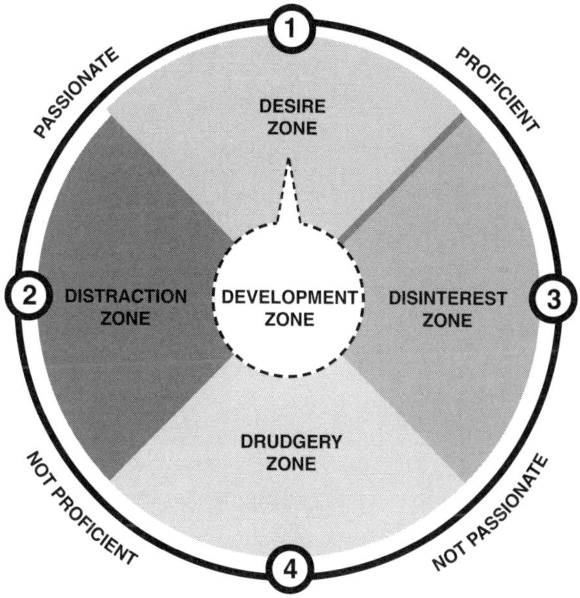

Courtesy Michael Hyatt and his book,
Free to Focus: A Total Productivity System to Achieve More by Doing Less.

move puts them in a job they'll likely hate and therefore do poorly in. When your business is small, you will have many demands on your team members, and they won't be able to specialize or scale yet. But as you grow, the Freedom Compass gives you direction with the team so you can evolve down a path where the role each team member plays aligns with their Desire Zone. Nothing is ever perfect, but using the Freedom Compass to see where your team members are and where they want to be is a great exercise for self-awareness.

Each of us must be clear about what we do best and what brings us the most joy. That is a huge part of scale.

CHAPTER 8
TRANSFORMATIONAL TAKEAWAYS

- Optimizing your time allows you to focus on tasks that will be most important as you move toward the Green Line.
- Make better use of your time by:

    1. Understanding time and value are a simple equation
    2. Identifying where your time is really being spent
    3. Knowing the average value of an hour of your time in a year
    4. Understanding the value of an hour of your time based on your current role and responsibilities

- Once you understand the principles of time, you must:

    1. Find the value of each task that you do for your business
    2. Focus on high-value tasks only, and leverage the rest

- Scalable businesses apply the Time–Value Principle to everyone in the company.
- Time is a moving target, and your highest-value tasks will shift as your business grows.
- Use the Freedom Compass to better identify your teams optimal roles and responsibilities.

9

DELEGATE WITH CONFIDENCE

It'll take more time to explain how to do this than to do it myself.

— Top advisor

Chapter 9 Transformational Targets

- Learn the differences between temporary and permanent delegation and how each affects your business and your team.
- Change the way you approach meetings by using them to determine a delegation life cycle.
- Use The Delegation Life Cycle to decide where to delegate tasks.

My friend Ron had a business with about thirty teammates. He once told me that early on in the business, he had a hard time delegating. This is not uncommon. Delegation is something most business owners struggle with. At first, Ron said he held onto most of the work he could have delegated to others—things like putting together forty seminar packets, boxing them up, and driving them to the location. When he did assign tasks, they were usually minor things that needed to be done around the office. Because Ron was so uncomfortable delegating, he introduced each assignment by saying, "Will you do me a quick favor?" Then he handed off the task.

As Ron's business grew, he realized this tactic wasn't working. At first, teammates were eager to help the boss any way they could. However, over time, they realized that when Ron asked for help, it was sure to be something unimportant. Subtle clues such as slumping their shoulders when they walked away or responding to his task more quietly led Ron to believe that they actually resented being asked to help, and he was right. All of them had begun to feel like glorified personal assistants rather than valued team members who could be trusted with greater responsibilities. Fortunately, Ron figured out what he was doing wrong before completely alienating his workforce. His casual approach to delegation was flawed in two ways, which he later shared with me.

1. Ron treated his teammates as servants.

By keeping all the high-leverage work for himself—meeting with clients, developing marketing campaigns—Ron silently communicated a lack of trust in his team members. Asking them, "Will you do me a favor?" only drove the point home. Ron had unwittingly cast himself in the role of the genius with a thousand helpers, as business leader and author Jim Collins puts it. Ron did all the real work. His teammates were there to handle the scut work he either couldn't be bothered with or didn't have time for. The teammates wanted to help, but they felt unempowered.

Fortunately, Ron came to see that teammates don't work for the boss; they work for the business. They aren't there to do little "favors" for the owner. They signed on to do important work that will advance the vision of the company. Team members actually want responsibility. They come to a company hoping to make a meaningful contribution and to grow professionally with that company. Every teammate wants to make a meaningful contribution in a space where they can use their area of expertise to deliver results.

Delegation is never a personal favor to the leader. It's a way to give clear direction to team members so they can maximize the value of their contribution while learning and growing at the same time. A new person with very little experience may be handed lower value tasks but as they progress so will their responsibilities. This is a natural progression and development that occurs on all teams, but we do not want high-value people taking on low-value tasks. They don't want it. We as a business don't want it either. Remember, you don't want a thousand helpers. You want a

Remember, you don't want a thousand helpers. You want a thousand great team members on the mission you have developed.

thousand great team members on the mission you have developed.

2. Ron believed his teammates served the boss, not the vision of the company.

Because Ron initially assumed that his teammates served him personally, he totally missed the flipside of the delegation equation—that his job was to serve them.

When you get on the Green Line, your business will become less dependent on you over time. That means its growth will depend more and more on the productivity of your team. You can't achieve scale on your own. No leader can. Your job is to bring the vision and then inspire and equip the team. The teammates actually do the work of scaling the business. As they grow both in competence and in number, your business will grow.

What do good teammates want?

1. **Pride in what they're doing**
2. **Growth–they never want to feel stuck or like an order taker**
3. **A career path, not a job**

That's exactly what good teammates want. They want to take on more responsibility and develop greater skills. They want to get more out of their careers, just like you do. So when you have a limited view of what delegation is and how it works, you limit your team, and as a result, you limit your business. Poor delegation kills their motivation, decreases their effort, and undermines the vision. When you look at each teammate as a capable, trustworthy team member who wants the business to grow just as much as you do, you'll do everything you can to equip them and turn them loose. And you'll be amazed at what they can do. The leader's job is to empower the team. The more successful your team is, the more successful your company will be.

The Delegation Life Cycle

Over time you want to delegate responsibilities, not tasks. Once you start delegating responsibilities, you can then move toward delegating thinking. In other words, your team will eventually start problem-solving for you, which will take another big time drain off your plate.

This is what I call The Delegation Life Cycle, and it looks like this:

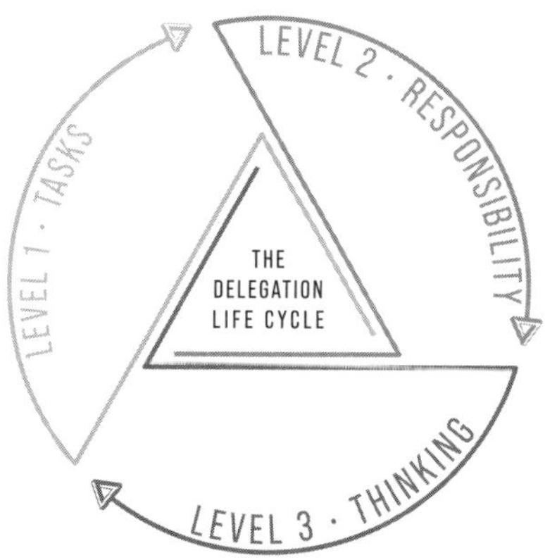

This pathway gears up your team to excel at what they do best: get excited about their jobs, and free you up to do your highest-level tasks. There is no "I" in scale; it's a team sport, and you've got to let your team play. No matter how hard you work, you can't scale your business by yourself. Your success depends on the growth of your team. To get the best from your team, you must become a great delegator and leader.

Right now, you may feel a bit like Ron did when he started his business. He knew he wasn't a great delegator. In fact, he was a little timid about it at first. And like Ron, you may have had some failed attempts at delegating work to teammates. Or, like Mike who we talked about in Chapter 8—specifically how he had trouble delegating his low-value tasks to other teammates—you may be holding onto work that could easily be delegated because you fear it won't be done as well as you could do it yourself. That's an understandable fear, but it's a misplaced one.

Anyone can learn to delegate well using the techniques I'll show you in this chapter. Even if you've failed at this in the past, delegation is a skill you can master. And it's essential for you to learn. Spending your time on low-revenue tasks you don't enjoy is a clear recipe for burnout. To get on the Green Line, scale your business, and achieve your vision, you must become a master delegator. You can do that by learning the following strategies for delegation.

1. Permanent delegation vs. temporary delegation
2. Curriculum training vs. situational training
3. The 10-80-10 rule

1. Permanent Delegation vs. Temporary Delegation

The chief complaint from advisors who are on the Red Line is this: "I don't have enough time."

That's because they need to learn how to delegate tasks so they can free up time for their highest priorities. There's no other way for the business to scale. Ironically, their chief objection to delegating tasks sounds exactly the same: "I don't have enough time." Advisors fear that if they delegate, the quality of work will drop, and the work won't get done. But they are also great at talking themselves into just doing whatever the task is—themselves. In fact, I often hear advisors say something like this: "It'll take more time to explain how to do this than to do it myself." Sound familiar?

Why don't people delegate? Three reasons:

1. **Fear of decreased quality**
2. **Fear that it won't get done**
3. **Convinced they can do it alone**

When people say this, it's a sure sign that they're thinking of delegation as a temporary solution. In their minds, they're doing the same thing Ron did with his teammates—asking for a one-off favor to save a little time on a busy day. Certainly, there is a place for one-time task assignments. But that's not the secret to recouping hours of your time each week. The only way to solve the problem of not having enough time is to take the time to permanently delegate tasks to someone else. That way, the task never returns to you. It's no longer your responsibility. That means not only delegating the work but also the responsibility for it. That clears both your desk and your mental space, allowing you to concentrate on your highest-leverage work. Permanent delegation may take longer on the front end, but it pays huge dividends down the road.

Here's an example. Imagine that you are the first one in line to receive client service requests. You may have a staff member help with a request here or there, but you do most of that work yourself. How long might that take you? Four hours a week? Maybe six? It's true that your clients get the feeling that you're personally interested in helping them, but at the end of the day, the solution to their problem would be the same whether you were involved or not. So that brief contact with those clients is costing you perhaps $6,000 per week, using the sample values from the last chapter. This is a prime example of stepping over dollars to pick up pennies.

Now imagine what your week would look like if you trained team members to be fully responsible for service work. They would be first in line to resolve customer service issues. And they would be fully responsible for the outcome. You would seldom—or never—be involved. By doing this, you would literally replace yourself as first in line, and your team could then involve you only as needed. Think about that last statement. That's you serving your staff rather than your team serving you, which is exactly how to scale your business. They are in charge, they own the role, and they will determine when to bring you into the game. You don't have to think about it or worry about it at all. They own it and actually play the role of protecting your time. See the difference?

Permanent delegation involves delegating both the work and the responsibility of the outcome, and you can't do that with someone who hasn't been trained. There are few things more frustrating for a team member than to be given work and be held accountable for the results without having the skills or information required to succeed. That only produces stress. To delegate permanently, you must invest time in training. When a team member has confidence that they can succeed in a role, they will take ownership of it. And that's what frees up your time and helps scale the business.

It may take days or perhaps weeks to train a team member to the point where they can accept this kind of responsibility. But when you do, the work will be off your plate for good. The better you communicate the role and the outcomes, the more confident you both will be with transferring the responsibility. Don't be afraid to give up control. Don't worry that the quality of service will drop. The only reason you feel that way now is because you haven't fully trained someone to accept the responsibility, which includes monitoring their progress at the start. If you are overly cautious about giving up control, it shows you have not fully trained your staff.

Permanent delegation involves delegating both the work and the responsibility of the outcome, and you can't do that with someone who hasn't been trained.

2. Curriculum Training vs. Situational Training

Broadly speaking, there are two approaches to training a team member to accept a responsibility—situational training and curriculum training. Situational training can be compared to on-the-job training. In the case of handling customer service requests, that would equate to the teammate shadowing you for a while as you handle requests. In time, they would see most of the situations you deal with concerning client service. After a while, they will remember what to do in each situation. Then you might allow them to handle some requests while you shadow them. In time, you'd both have confidence that they could handle 99 percent of the requests they will face. This is the most common type of training for advisors. However, situational training alone is not the ideal approach. Here's why.

By relying on situational training, there is a multitude of different situations that your team member will have to experience. There may be thousands of little things they need to observe. Asking them to comprehend, experience, and learn each of these things is a big ask. I think of school as an example. Imagine your college professor going in front of your class each day for a semester but not giving you any books, workbooks, or outlines. Then, at the end of the semester, your professor gives you a test about everything they've said and expects you to remember it all. What's the probability that you will pass that test? Now flip the example around, and imagine the professor providing you curriculum to follow and then giving you the test. You could study the materials, review them, and increase the likelihood that you'll actually learn the material and pass the test.

By creating a core curriculum for your team members to train with over time, you increase their chances of success and the speed at which they can learn and contribute. And you've also provided them with the situational experience.

I think of my business of coaching advisors as another example.

I have completed more than 40,000 hours coaching financial advisors. There is no way I could communicate all I've learned to someone else in a short period of time and expect them to succeed. There are just too many different situations to explain. I'd have to create a curriculum in order to do that. Intentional curriculum training can give a new team member 90 percent of what they need to know in order to be successful. However, the last 10 percent of what they need to know might take a lifetime to learn since there are so many unique situations that arise over time.

That's the shortcoming of situational training. It takes a good deal of time, and even then it is not complete. Because experience is the only teacher, the training can't be complete until the learner has faced every possible experience, and those experiences are constantly evolving. Unfortunately, most advisors really don't have the time to train teammates using only the situational training technique. They resort to brain dumping all they know about the task and then letting the teammates sink or swim with the new responsibility. Often this leaves advisors wondering, "Why haven't they learned it?" Not surprisingly, that approach is prone to failure.

Curriculum training is a much more reliable training technique. This is a systematic approach to training that uses written or online content to guide the trainee through the basics of the work, including how to handle core situations. Rather than doing the brain dump and saying, "Good luck!" the leader develops a written guide for teammates to follow.

Don't be intimidated by the word curriculum. Remember, when you prepared for tests, you usually had something on hand as a basis for studying. That might have been a textbook, a workbook, an online course, or training videos. Either way, you knew you could pass the test if you put in the effort to learn that material.

That's what I mean by curriculum. It's the training content a teammate can master in order to succeed in their role.

A beautiful thing about curriculum training is that if you do have a staff member leave, anybody can fill their shoes quickly because they have the manual on how to succeed in that role. Documenting your processes is critical to scale, and it honestly doesn't take that long when you do it with intention.

A beautiful thing about curriculum training is that if you do have a staff member leave, anybody can fill their shoes quickly because they have the manual on how to succeed in that role.

Once your staff has been trained by you along with the curriculum, they will still need your help with situational guidance. But that will be much less frequent. Rather than needing your help for let's say 90 percent of the role, they may need you only for the last 10 percent of training. Even that will rapidly decrease over time.

3. The 10-80-10 Rule

Once your staff has been trained by you along with the curriculum, they will still need your help with situational guidance. But it will be much less frequent, as the core roles have been carefully trained. You still have to address the fears—that delegating means you'll lose control of your company, that work quality will decrease, that whoever is doing the task won't follow through.

Most entrepreneurs have experienced these situations. They delegate, thinking something is getting done, just to find out it vanished into thin air. Then they have to follow up and see what happened. You can completely eliminate those fears by using the 10-80-10 Rule.

I learned this concept from Michael Hyatt, a master at delegation. Quite simply, the 10-80-10 Rule means you involve yourself in the first 10 percent of the project and the last 10 percent, but you leave the middle 80 percent to your team. In other words, you set a clear vision on the front end and allow your team to execute within those parameters. Toward the end, you become involved again to do a quality check and make any adjustments that might be needed before launch.

VISION	EXECUTION	QUALITY CONTROL
10 —	80 —	10

This rule pairs the concepts of leverage and delegation to ensure you get more done in less time while maintaining the quality you envision. It's the perfect approach for one-time projects and for those advisors who are nervous about handing off control of an important responsibility to others. We use this method frequently in the Triad office to move projects along quickly as we grow while maintaining executive oversight.

Oversight is the key. That's different from control and even more effective. One of the most common complaints I hear from advisors and staff members is that the quality drops when they hand off a task. That does happen, of course, so this fear of delegation becomes an enemy of scale. Having been burned by one or two projects that didn't turn out as intended, advisors typically suck back all tasks and hold them close. As a result, the business simply cannot grow.

I've found that in most cases when delegation fails, it's the fault of the person delegating, not the person doing the task. Most often the breakdown comes in either the first 10 percent of the work or the last 10 percent. Either the delegator didn't make their expectations clear at the outset, or they neglected to check in at the end to answer questions, verify the outcome, or make adjustments. Delegating a task does not mean you can drop it like a bomb and run away. It involves setting clear expectations at the outset and checking on results near the end. Many entrepreneurs are running so fast that they fail to follow through on the first and last 10 percent. That sets the team member up for failure.

I've found that in most cases when delegation fails, it's the fault of the person delegating, not the person doing the task.

The First 10 Percent

With delegation, quality is a direct result of clarity. To get quality at the end, you must provide clarity at the beginning. So the first 10 percent of the task is vision. This is where you give clear direction for the results and the parameters you expect. It means describing what the result should look like and giving the team member the why behind it so they see where this fits into the big picture. It's really hard to move forward in any role without the context and conviction of what it's about. So, over communicate on the front end, and make sure whatever you're trying to achieve includes a framework that's been agreed upon by the whole team.

Next, there are only three actions that should be taken once the first 10 percent has been delivered.

1. **They can take action.** This only works when they are 100 percent clear on what needs to be done. Only then can you move to execution and start building.
2. **They can ask questions.** Once you've shared the first 10 percent, just because you think they understand the task doesn't necessarily meant that they do. Give them plenty of time to ask questions so that they have a clear understanding of expectations.
3. **They can honestly disagree with the vision or something that's part of the process.** You want your team to have conviction, and if they're thinking "we are thinking about this the wrong way," let them share that. This is an absolutely acceptable response. Sometimes the leader is wrong, and you want open communication and feedback. Once again, you want your team to have the conviction to go forward and build without hesitation, and if they aren't confident or are

questioning it, you won't get the outcome you want.

The Middle 80 Percent

The middle 80 percent is execution, or time for your team to build what you've envisioned. This is where the teammates take ownership, exercise initiative, express creativity, and produce results. The first and last 10 percent are always exciting to the person who delegated the work, but the middle 80 percent is where the person doing the work gets to shine. Of course, they may come back with some questions, and you are there to help them or serve them if needed. But now it's their primary responsibility, not yours, to follow through. Often, new questions will come up as work is in progress. But since they now own the task, the questions should be about gaining greater clarity on expectations or resources. Your role in this stage is simply to help them as needed.

The Final 10 Percent

The final 10 percent is the quality check. Here you come back into the process so the teammate can present their work. At this stage, you still have time to make adjustments to ensure the result is exactly as you envisioned it and the quality is right. If you've both done your jobs well, the result will be very close to what you had in mind. If not, it's not a problem because you've planned for revisions and tweaks in your process. The team member can revise as needed, which will be a learning experience for both of you. The next time around, you'll better understand how to communicate your expectations, and your teammate will have a better idea of the questions to ask during the vision-casting stage. Once the adjustments are complete, you'll have exactly what you wanted with only a 20 percent involvement in the process.

Typically, after a role has been run through like this a few times, the teammate starts to get it, and the overall role becomes permanently delegated and in their wheelhouse. There may have been a lot of questions the first time or two, but eventually, they will fully get it. And you have complete confidence in them as well, so you can give up control.

Imagine repeating this process over and over with various projects.

- How much of your time could you reclaim if team members were able to do 80 percent of your project work up front—then over time they own it 100 percent?
- What could you accomplish if you knew the quality of these projects would not be diminished by delegating them to a staff member?
- What could your current staff achieve if they were given more and more opportunities to handle work that only you have been able to do—until now?

Delegation will exponentially increase your productivity as well as your team members' productivity. And that's what it takes to scale your business.

Move through the Delegation Life Cycle—Tasks, Responsibilities, and Thinking

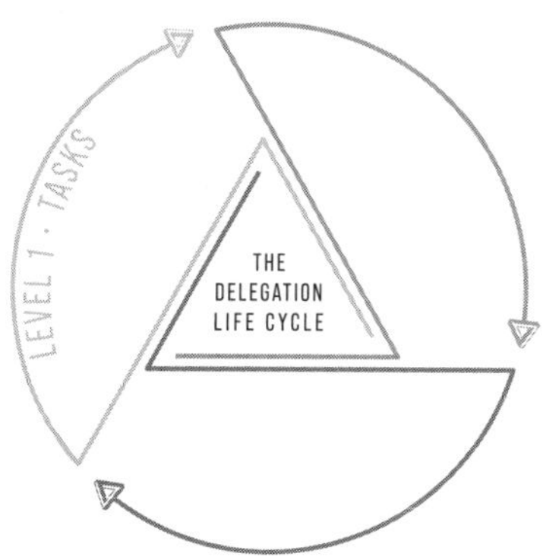

So far, we've talked about three strategies for delegation. You've probably been thinking about the many tasks you'd like to move off of your plate. Most likely, you're thinking in terms of tasks. That's the starting point for delegation—having someone else complete a task or assignment that you would otherwise do yourself. As we've seen, that can save you a great deal of labor over time. Investing the few hours it might take to delegate the task, including creating any curriculum you might need, is really an investment in yourself. Assigning tasks is level-one delegation, and it's the first step in the Delegation Life Cycle.

There are two additional levels of delegation, and they are much more powerful than delegating tasks. They are delegating responsibilities and delegating thinking.

Delegating Responsibilities

When you delegate responsibilities, you assign a higher level of authority to your teammates. You empower them not merely to return a phone call or follow up on a client request but also release responsibility to them to manage an area of work. When a teammate screens your calls, that saves you a certain amount of time, perhaps an hour or two a day. That's a great task to delegate. But what happens when you take that a step further and assign responsibility for communicating on your behalf? Then you leverage that teammate's contribution at a much higher level.

Now, rather than simply listening to your voicemail or reading your emails to determine which items require your response, the team member has the responsibility to respond to those messages, following the protocols you've taught them. That saves even more of your time, and it has the benefit of developing the teammate's skills and judgment. As I've mentioned before, great teammates want a career path, not a job. They want responsibility over time and the opportunity to continue to grow professionally. This is a path in order to do that.

Delegating a task says, "Here, handle this, and it'll save me fifteen minutes or an hour." Delegating responsibility says, "This belongs to you. I trust you to handle it as you think best. And you'll be responsible for the results."

Delegating responsibility saves you days or weeks, not merely hours, and it lets your teammate completely own the responsibility.

Delegating Thinking

The highest level of delegation is delegating thinking. It's a way to leverage not just your teammate's time or judgment but also their insight and creativity.

Much of the work we do involves problem-solving, which requires thinking through questions such as how to structure a marketing funnel, what would be the next skill to hire, or whether to diversify a product offering. These are not the kind of things that can be done in an hour or even an afternoon. They require

deep thought, discussion, reading, learning, and processing. They involve thinking, and this type of work is the highest level of delegation.

Think of the three levels of delegation in the Delegation Life Cycle like this: the Doer does the task, the Director owns responsibility of the outcome, and the Dreamer owns the thinking.

When you have trained teammates so they can bear some of the load through studying, strategizing, and problem-solving, you've reached delegation level three. These teammates are the brains behind the responsibility and are empowered to think about it so you don't have to. This is the point where your team members become partners in running the business. They think about the challenges of the present and the opportunities of the future.

Leveraging time saves you hours. Leveraging judgment saves you days or weeks. But leveraging thought and creativity can shave years off the time it would take to scale your business if you based it on your brain power alone.

Get Out of the Way

One of the best pieces of advice I received about scale came from an advisor who is literally an icon in the industry. He said the key is to hire great people and then get out of their way. Using 10-80-10 allows you to do this while still ensuring that you aren't just blindly setting up your business for failure. Through 10-80-10 you can get out of their way but still review and modify during the last 10 percent. There will be more on this in the Section 7, Culture. For now, let's just acknowledge that it is hard for advisors to evolve and transition, especially those who started in the business doing it all. But once you make the shift in mindset, you will be unstoppable, and there will be no limit to what you can accomplish.

#DBDL

When you embrace the fact that delegation is key to scale and start doing it like a pro, you will find it highly addictive. You will be blown away with how much more gets done than you ever thought possible. You will find yourself hyperfocused on bringing on great team members and seeing that they are properly prepared to accept responsibility. And you'll have incredible confidence as you move through the Delegation Life Cycle and get out of the way to watch these people flourish.

Chapter 9
Transformational Takeaways

- There are three strategies for delegation.
- Temporary delegation eliminates small tasks over short periods of time. Permanent delegation frees up your time over the long term and shifts responsibilities to teammates.
- Curriculum training is much more effective for permanent delegation.
- Ultimately you should spend 10 percent on the front end and 10 percent on the backend of projects with your team performing the middle 80 percent of responsibilities.
- The Delegation Life Cycle moves team members through levels of delegation. These levels include:
  - Tasks
  - Responsibilities
  - Thinking
- The only way to scale is to delegate to empower your team, and then get out of their way!

Looking to set your operations mindset for scale? Check out additional resources here.

SECTION 5
MARKETING

Now that you have the operations of your business set to scale, it's time to add fuel to your growth. Marketing is that fuel.

Marketing isn't about shiny objects or just getting people to come see you. It's about attracting the right people who you can best help. So, the best marketers in our industry get two things right. One, they market in a way that's authentic to them. Two, they build their marketing strategy and plan based on who they want to become and what they want to be known for long term.

Now that you have a vision, you have the clarity needed to build a solid marketing strategy.

Marketing isn't about shiny objects or just getting people to come see you. It's about attracting the right people who you can best help.

Too many people in every industry—not just ours—make two huge mistakes when it comes to marketing. One, they market in a way that is not at all authentic to them. Two, their marketing efforts don't support who they want to be in the long run. That is where vision and brand work together.

When you have a vision, you move from just throwing shiny objects out there as a marketing strategy to having a brand marketing strategy. Brand marketing sells a distinctive company with a definitive vision and unique products to an ideal customer. It does not sell something everyone else has—something from an indistinct company or brand—to anyone who will buy.

One of the advisors I work with is passionate about helping people protect their hard-earned money. His parents had their retirement taken from them due to bad advice and risking money they didn't have to lose. So today, rather than all things financial planning, that's what he has been called to do. It's what he focuses on in his business, and it's what he talks about in his marketing because that is his unique brand.

He doesn't switch his focus to managing risk assets after hearing that another advisor is having success with that approach, nor does he start talking about Social Security during seminars because he hears it's the new trend.

He remains authentic to himself, his vision, and his brand at all times…and it works.

People are craving a vision, a mission, and a purpose they can latch onto. A surface-level method of conducting business is not

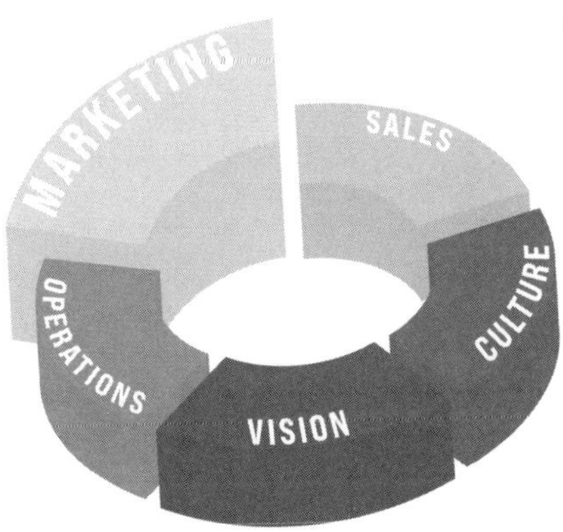

enough. You capture their hearts when you are authentic and have a deeper meaning around your identity.

When you're marketing to scale, you have a brand manifesto that is the path that guides you and keeps you accountable for what you should and should not do. This will keep you from latching onto shiny objects that are not right for your brand, your vision, and your business. It will also allow you to focus on strategy and tactics. In the end, this is what will save you from becoming another commodity in this industry.

In this section, you will learn how to:

- Change your mindset toward marketing
- Find your voice and differentiate
- Develop a marketing strategy that is then supported by marketing tactics
- Consistently align your brand with your vision and your marketing efforts
- Create a differentiated, congruent brand that targets your ideal audience

Are you ready for your next step toward unlimited growth, freedom, and joy?

10

SHIFTING YOUR MARKETING MINDSET

Shawn, the biggest change for me is when I realized the biggest factor in growing my business wasn't the planning, service, or the help I provided. I had all of that, but it didn't matter because I didn't have new clients to present it to. I began to see that if I really wanted to grow, I had to learn marketing.

—Top advisor

Chapter 10 Transformational Targets

- Change your marketing mindset. Done well, marketing isn't an expense. It's fuel for your business.
- Create a consistent marketing strategy so that you avoid chasing tactics.
- Learn to reverse engineer your marketing strategy so that you can match your marketing investment against desired outcomes.

Michael had been an advisor for more than twenty years. He loved the business, was passionate about helping people, and appreciated his clients more than anything. Michael was also a great advisor. He went above and beyond with every client, providing a very high level of service and planning. His business had grown steadily over a number of years, and very few advisors matched his attention to detail and devotion to client success. Michael's clients were raving fans of his work.

Yet Michael began to notice that many other advisors were growing their businesses at a much faster rate than he was. One year at an industry conference, the top advisors were recognized for their success. Michael was proud to be recognized for a great year, but this pride quickly faded as he realized he wasn't near the top of the list as he had once been. Even more disheartening, he noticed that advisors much younger than he was—who had far less experience—were walking across the stage to be recognized for higher performances. One of these young advisors had been in business for only three years yet was twice as productive as Michael. "How can this kid be beating my numbers?" Michael thought. "It took me twenty years to reach this point!"

Michael's thinking quickly went to an unhealthy place where he found plenty of excuses. He found himself creating a negative narrative about the situation, one where these younger achievers must be taking shortcuts or using unethical practices. Or maybe they were in a more affluent area, which gave them a competitive advantage.

Mastering the basics of the business and reaching a level of success paved the way for Michael to have an overconfident, prideful attitude and ultimately a terrible excuse for why someone else could be doing better than he was. When you know you're good at what you do, it's hard to believe that anyone with less skill or experience could do it better. But success is neither an entitlement nor an end point where you have arrived. It's an ongoing journey of growth. What got you to one level of achievement may not get you to the next. Ego is the enemy of scale, but ego is easy to miss. If you're approaching conversations and decisions with excuses, arrogance, or the feeling of knowing what does and doesn't work, you're letting your ego limit what you can become. An attitude of humility leads to discovery, and that fuels learning and growth. Ego is a huge enemy of scale.

Ego is the enemy of scale,
but ego is easy to miss.

Fortunately, Michael recognized that the negative narrative he had adopted would not help him grow. He was able to regain the day-one mindset of a student at the beginning of his career. He began to ask himself a more empowering question: "What do these young advisors know that I don't?" It didn't take long for Michael to realize that he needed to put his ego aside and talk to some of those advisors to see what he could learn.

As Michael began to engage with those advisors, he quickly discovered what was fueling their remarkable success. He applied what he learned to his own business, and it started to grow almost immediately. Within twelve months, he had nearly doubled his previous business. Best of all, he was helping even more people than he ever thought possible.

I observed Michael's breakout year and couldn't wait to sit down with him and talk about it. I wanted to hear every little detail of what he had discovered that led to these amazing results. As we met over coffee, he told me the breakthrough was rather simple.

"Shawn," Michael said, "the biggest change for me is when I realized the biggest factor in growing my business wasn't the planning, service, or help I provided. I had all of that, but it didn't matter because I didn't have new clients to present it to. I began to see that if I really wanted to grow, I had to learn marketing. Product knowledge and client services are not enough. I had to get good at marketing as well."

And there it was, the discovery that took Michael twenty years to learn but less than twelve months to apply. Marketing is not optional. It is a key factor to scaling your business. Advisors who move from the Red Line to the Green Line understand this:

1. Marketing is required to truly scale.
2. Marketing isn't a short-term tactic; it's a long-term strategy.
3. Marketing is an investment, not an expense.
4. Marketing is carefully built.
5. Marketing is consistent and congruent.
6. Marketing is intentional.

Marketing Is Required to Truly Scale

For the first twenty years of his career, Michael did what a lot of new advisors do. He focused on the basics of the financial services business—portfolio management, sales processes, business processes, operations, and client experience. These things were the essence of his business, so they were critical areas of focus for a new advisor. And they worked—up to a certain point.

Michael had gotten a lot of business through his warm market—people he knew or who knew him. That allowed him to grow through word of mouth from his existing relationships. That was enough to keep his business growing consistently. He also dabbled in marketing from time to time but never felt the urgency to make it a key element of his business plan. Every once in a while, he latched onto a marketing idea—there certainly wasn't any shortage of opportunities—and went for it.

Michael could recall any number of times that a conference presenter or marketing representative had offered to spearhead a marketing campaign. But they were expensive and seemed so uncertain. Michael brushed most of them aside, seeing them as risky expenditures rather than investments in the future of his business. There were a lot of reasons not to invest in marketing, and he let those excuses handicap the growth of his business.

It took seeing younger advisors who were outproducing him for Michael to realize that all this hard work and planning would make no impact if he wasn't able to reach new clients with his offering. Marketing would connect him with the people he wanted to serve. Marketing would spearhead the growth of his business. Marketing was essential for scale.

Michael's mistake is one I've seen hundreds of advisors make. They focus on products and service, which is the heart of their offering to the public. But they neglect the one thing necessary to connect them to the people they desire to serve—marketing. A great advisor without a great marketing plan will always be the best-kept secret in town. To scale your business, you must take marketing seriously. Marketing is the fuel for growth.

> A great advisor without a great marketing plan will always be the best-kept secret in town.

Marketing Isn't a Short-Term Tactic; It's a Long-Term Strategy

Another common mistake I see is when financial advisors treat marketing as a short-term tactic rather than a long-term strategy. You need both, and they are very different.

Attend any industry conference, and you'll hear lots of talk about the latest marketing ideas. These conversations can be useful—to a degree. But often, they serve as a distraction more than anything else. Here's the key. Marketing activities must be tied to an overall marketing strategy to truly work. Looking for the next big trend or no-fail tactic is a waste of time without an overarching strategy for identifying prospects and moving them through a process—a funnel, if you will—that brings them to the point of sale. Tactics alone produce limited results. Most of them become a flavor of the month that makes the rounds in the industry and is then discarded. What you need are the elements of

> "Strategy without tactics is the slowest route to victory. Tactics without strategy is the noise before defeat."
>
> —Sun Tzu

a solid marketing strategy. Any number of tactics may be effective for one aspect of the strategy or another. Tactics come and go, but a solid marketing strategy will fuel your growth for a long time.

We'll learn more about marketing strategy in the following chapters. For now, let's keep focusing on the mental shift needed to move from seeing marketing as an afterthought to seeing it as a core activity for scaling your business.

Marketing Is an Investment, Not an Expense

Most advisors think of marketing as an expense ("Wow! That costs a lot!") and a risky one at that. Marketing does cost money. There's no doubt about that. And for most marketing tactics that you're familiar with, that investment is risky. It's possible to spend a lot of money on a marketing campaign and see little or no results from it. Campaigns can be viewed as a test for you and your business—sometimes they work, and other times they don't. Over time, you really want to minimize the damage of failed tests and maximize the fuel with those that work.

But you don't want to let caution or fear of failure to handicap your ability to grow your business. A long-term marketing strategy means that some of your marketing will do great, and some will fail. But overall, we will learn, and it will net a huge positive over time.

If you go into marketing with the attitude of "I'll give it a shot," you're already setting yourself up for a plan that won't work. There are two ways to approach a marketing plan when you go into it. What if it doesn't work? What if it does? Those are two ways to see the same dilemma, and a company set to scale asks the latter.

Long-term strategy keeps the business's vision in mind. The long-term vision knows that marketing must be an integral part of the business, and it takes that seriously in order to build it right. With this in mind, even if some marketing efforts fail, you can identify what you learned and then determine how to improve. Great marketing is not bought or done off the side of the desk. It's built very intentionally.

Over time, a solid marketing strategy will generate predictable growth and bring people into your office consistently. That means you'll be able to predict the number of new clients you'll sign and the worth of those new customers based on the resources you put into the marketing system. You will be able to tie every dollar spent on marketing back into an ROI in future earnings for your company. That will help with budgeting, forecasts, and everything else as you grow.

Think about it this way. If you went to Las Vegas and walked into a casino, you might put a couple of dollars in a flashy slot machine in front of you. You put a dollar in, you pull the lever, and bam! You win! The slot machine gives you $5 back. Inspired by

> Over time, a solid marketing strategy will generate predictable growth and bring people into your office consistently.

that quick win, you might try it again. Let's say you put another dollar in, and again the slot machine gives you $5 back. Over the next hour, you find that every time you put a dollar in, you get $5 back. If that happened to you, how fast would you fund that machine, knowing it was almost certain to produce a 5:1 return on investment? I suspect you'd shovel in dollars as fast as you could.

A slot machine would certainly not give you that kind of ROI. But money spent on marketing can if it's built correctly, and it will work that way when you take it seriously and make it a truly critical component of your business. With a solid marketing strategy, you will know exactly how much money you put in. Based on that investment—not expense—you can roughly predict how much you will get back in return.

That means when your accounting team meets with you and points out that you went over budget on marketing expenses, you'll be able to show them how that spending is directly tied to revenue at a return ratio of 5:1, or whatever your consistent yield turns out to be. Marketing is not a normal expense. An expense is a pure cost. If it's done correctly, marketing is an investment. If you have an effective marketing plan, the more you spend on marketing, the more your revenue will grow.

To put it another way, if you knew your marketing system generated $500,000 in annual revenue for every $100,000 invested, then not spending that $100,000 on marketing would be the most expensive decision you could make. It would cost your company $400,000.

How much money are you losing every single day by not implementing a strategic marketing plan?

And if you really want to grow, you've got to be great at marketing. If you choose not to market your business because it's too expensive, you are actually choosing not to scale your growth since you are lacking the fuel to do it.

Marketing Is Carefully Built

Many advisors approach marketing based on emotion or as a quick idea to pull the trigger on. What I mean is that they get excited about marketing their business after some inspiring event or milestone and decide to go for it. "If it worked for one person," they think, "it will work for me." It's like ready, fire, aim opposed to ready, aim, fire.

What's the likelihood that you'll hit your target?

What another advisor may have done to get a marketing initiative to work isn't going to work for you if you just point and shoot. You've got to understand all the little details behind that strategy and then build the marketing activities to support it correctly.

Years ago at a large conference, a hero was on stage who said that one of their best marketing initiatives was radio. They wowed the crowd, and every advisor said, "I've got to start doing radio."

A lot of them had the courage to go forward, pay the money, and show up to start the radio initiative. Then they held their breath, hoping it would work.

In the end, the large majority found it didn't work for them.

Why?

They hadn't learned all the little details about radio that the hero had learned and then put into place to make radio work.

Which stations and time slots would best capture the ears of their ideal audience?

What was the price per listener, and how would that impact ROI?

Should they do ads, a radio show, or a combination of both?

What message should they share to get people to reach out and contact them?

Once calls came in, how should the team handle those calls? How could they increase the odds that they would meet the lead in the office for the right reasons?

These little details matter, and you can't just "buy" effective marketing. You have to build it within your business in order for it to work.

Marketing Is Consistent and Congruent

A short-sighted marketing strategy leads to stress, frustration, and lost momentum. It's common for people to think and act this way. For example, advisors set goals at the start of the year and determine that this year they're going to really get serious about growing the business. So they throw money at marketing ideas that seem like a really good idea without really thinking them through. Or they create a marketing strategy that creates a pathway for those tactics in order to support the overarching business goals. They might attend an industry event and get inspired by the success stories of the high achievers they meet. "Yes!" they think, "I'm going to kick my production into high gear!"

So they schedule a one-off marketing idea, hoping it works. Then they generate some meetings and see how they do. A few weeks later, they consider trying it again. When they have another lull in their schedule, they try it yet again.

A month or so later, they question whether the activity is truly helpful—do they want to deal with that anymore? They're tired. Although they have a hunch that it did or didn't bring in clients, they actually don't have real data to back up the total expense, the time it took, or the actual results. Based on that lack of information, they skip the next cycle of that marketing activity—and then another. Their approach was tied to the excitement of the moment or the bandwidth in an already busy schedule. Looking at marketing like a side project—one you'll do when you have time—is not how to scale. Short bursts of activity will never beat the results produced by a consistent marketing strategy.

Years ago, an advisor I worked with used the burst-of-energy approach. With adrenaline-fueled bursts of activity, he brought on a wave of new clients. But then there was a lull. He skipped a month or two of marketing and then ramped it up again. If he'd been able to bring in new clients consistently month after month, he would have easily doubled his business in a year. But his effort was always the result of a burst of his own energy, and he simply couldn't sustain that all year long.

The following year, I helped him create a marketing calendar for the upcoming twelve months. Together, we took the emotion out of his marketing efforts and simply followed the calendar of events we'd established for the year. The advisor never had to think about whether he had the energy to psych himself up for a marketing event. He simply did whatever was on the calendar. It made him accountable to follow through with his marketing strategy.

As you can imagine, this advisor was able to sustain this effort with great consistency. As a result, he more than doubled his income that year. This approach was better for his business and better for him personally since he didn't have to exert energy making marketing decisions every few weeks. It was also better for his team who could plan for events months in advance rather than scramble to pull together an event on short notice. Consistent effort beats a burst of energy every time.

Marketing Is Intentional

The final mental shift you need to make in order to effectively market your company is to begin by thinking about the outcome you want to achieve, not the resources you are willing to spend. In other words, you need to create your marketing plan based on the result, not the amount of time and money you happen to have available in any given month. You need to reverse engineer your marketing plan, working backward from your revenue goal.

As I've noted, most advisors view marketing as an expense and undertake it sporadically when they have bursts of energy or interest in growing their business. That leads to a short-term approach based on available resources. It begins by asking a question like this: "I have X dollars to spend and X hours to invest. What can I do with that?" This approach begins with the expenditure—money and time—and works forward to create an outcome. That simply furthers the sporadic, emotion-driven approach to marketing.

I mentioned the advisor I worked with who doubled his income after developing a consistent marketing strategy. What I haven't told you yet is how he and I created that marketing plan. First, we determined the outcome he wanted to achieve. He believed—and I agreed—that he could easily double his revenue in one year. Since we had a wealth of data from his existing business, we were able to work backward from that goal and calculate the activity that would be needed to reach it. Here are the actual numbers from that plan.

Goal:	**$50 million in new assets**
New clients needed	100
1st appt. to 2nd appt	10:6 (60%)
2nd appt to client	10:6 (66%)

From there it was a matter of simple arithmetic. Based on that data, we calculated that he had a 40 percent closing rate from the first appointment all the way through to a client. So to land 100 new clients, he had to generate around 250 prospects. His appointments took about one hour, so the breakdown went something like this:

1st appointments	250 hours
2nd appointments	150 hours
Annual total	**400 hours**

The key to hitting his goal was to spend 400 hours in front of prospective new clients during that year. Assuming a forty-hour work week and fifty weeks per year, he had about 2,000 hours of work available. By spending about 20 percent of his time—one day a week—on prospective clients, he could easily reach his goal by focusing on high-value activities. That would allow him to get more done in less time, which is the key to **#DBDL** and freedom. You keep moving up in value per hour and therefore produce more than you ever could have doing low-value stuff.

For this advisor, it all boiled down to generating five new prospect appointments per week. How would he generate those five appointments? This advisor was already having some success generating new clients by hosting events. So we started with that. How many first appointments did he generate per event? Once we had that number, which was easily available in his records, we knew exactly how many events he would need to host in order to reach his goal. From there, it was just a matter of working the plan, showing up every day, and doing whatever was on the calendar.

Obviously, he measured his marketing as he went and made slight adjustments to stay on track. But the question of "should I" or "should I not" was based on his plan. He had reverse engineered his way to success, beginning with the outcome he wanted to achieve. And as you can imagine, he hit his goal.

In my experience, when advisors begin their marketing plan by looking at the outcome they want to achieve and reverse engineer the process to meet that goal, they nearly always exceed the goal. Why? Because the more activity you put forward, the more people you see, the better you get, and the luckier you seem to get as well. You may wind up landing that incredibly large client who throws the numbers way up for the year. Or your marketing efforts may produce a brand recognition that generates new clients passively—they find you rather than you finding them. Either way, there is a compound effect from consistent marketing. You will nearly always reach your goal—and then some.

Start Now

In this business, everyone seems to be looking for a silver bullet. Advisors latch on to any idea that seems to be a quick fix or one-stop solution to bring new clients through the door. I can tell you that no such thing exists. There is no silver bullet. Good marketing is the result of consistent, strategic effort.

Remember Michael, the advisor who was at first jealous and then curious about the younger advisors who were outproducing him? As he started thinking about marketing more and more, he began to read books, pick up ideas from friends, and attend conferences about how to become a better marketer. Before long, he found himself inundated with great ideas and best practices he could model to build the marketing side of his business. Eventually, he created a marketing team whose number-one focus was to increase the number of new people he and his team saw each week.

Michael found that the more people his marketing team brought through the front door, the more people they were able to help achieve their financial goals and the greater impact they made. Along with that, of course, Michael and his teammates prospered. His only regret? "I just wish I would have learned all this sooner. I always wanted to reach more people, but I somehow focused all my time on everything but marketing."

You can learn from Michael's experience. Make marketing a core aspect of your business. Create a strategic plan to achieve your revenue goals, and then work it consistently. Your business will scale faster than you ever thought possible, and your impact will be greater than anything you have imagined.

Chapter 10
Transformational Takeaways

- Marketing isn't a tactic. It's a strategy and needs to be treated as such.
- Too many people view marketing as an expense. Yes, it costs money, but if done correctly, it's an investment, not an expense.
- You can reverse-engineer your marketing expense so you know exactly how much to invest in order to get the results you want.
- Your marketing strategy can't be based on bursts of emotional energy. Instead, it must be consistent.

11

REFINING YOUR MESSAGE: WHO ARE YOU?

Our business completely changed the moment we realized how to effectively message who we are and what we do.

— Top advisor

Chapter 11 Transformational Targets

- Decide how you're going to differentiate yourself from your competition—price doesn't count.
- Practice congruent marketing.
- Be your authentic self.

One of my advisors used to run joint seminars with an attorney. The attorney advertised the seminars around the topic of estate planning, and the advisor and the attorney split presentation time. My advisor saw a great opportunity to market his business and gladly agreed to the arrangement with the lawyer. The first seminar produced a solid turnout, and the lawyer and advisor split the presentation time as planned. The seminar went beautifully, and afterward my advisor was primed to work the audience, answer questions, and hopefully book a number of appointments. None of that happened.

As you would imagine, all the attendees wanted information on wills and trusts—core elements of estate planning. Unfortunately, estate planning was not a core element of this advisor's business. She was focused on investing and had little experience advising people on their legacy. So the advisor and her staff spent a fruitless half hour trying to convince people to meet with them about something they had no interest in.

The lawyer wound up booking a number of appointments, but the advisor came away almost empty-handed. The advisor's marketing message didn't align with her core business, her ideal client, or the product she had to offer. As a result, she generated very few appointments, and even those had a much lower-than-usual closing rate. This advisor stuck with the estate planning seminars a few more times before concluding that they were a wasted effort.

However, the results were great for the lawyer. He booked a number of appointments from each seminar, and the closing rate was sky high. Why? His marketing message aligned with his skills, product, and ideal customer. This experience was a costly mistake for my advisor, but it's one that you can easily avoid. The goal of marketing is to bring new leads in contact with your business and convert them to clients. To be effective in doing that, you must know what you stand for and what you have to offer your clients—two points of clarity that vision can help with.

When you know who you are and what you can offer your clients, you can create a marketing message that is differentiated, congruent, and targeted.

Differentiate

When all products (or services) are the same, the consumer will shop on price only. When you build a brand that attracts people to a certain more meaningful outcome than a product, they will pay more for that experience. Just look at hotels. They all have beds to sleep on so why do you pay premium prices for higher end hotels when you want to get away from it all? Experience. You want the experience of the excellent breakfast, the pool, the softer sheets, and the five-star service of the staff. Consumers' willingness to pay more for an experience transcends all industries, and the business that gets them to pay more wins because they have differentiated themselves from all the other commodities out there.

In any marketplace, you have to differentiate yourself from the competition in order to survive, let alone scale. This is a lesson many financial advisors have yet to learn. All of you "do" retirement planning. In fact, when most financial advisors are asked, "What can you do for me?" the answer is typically, "I can help you prepare for retirement." How does that make you any different than any other advisor? It doesn't.

As of 2021, there were roughly 300,000 financial advisors in the United States[10]. All of them can set you up with a 401(k).

10 https://www.financestrategists.com/financial-advisor/advisor-types/how-many-financial-advisors-are-in-the-us/

When you productize your unique value to your clients, you set yourself apart from every single one.

Long ago, the fast-food giants learned that the front end of their marketing had to be unique. They had to offer something nobody else had, whether that was a Big Mac, customized food, or fresh orders. They couldn't just sell hamburgers.

Most advisors only focus on investments and are known for being the investments "guy" or "gal." As vital as investments are to a retirement plan, the number one concern of retirees is "will I run out of money?"[11] How are you addressing income planning, and that need for your clients?

#DBDL

Investments are only one of five critical pieces to a full retirement plan. An entire plan should include investments, income planning, tax planning, health care planning, and estate planning. By including all five aspects in your planning process, you can differentiate yourself from the advisor who only address one or two aspects of a retirement plan.

To scale, you must take your unique approach and turn it into a product. You must answer the question, "What is my Big Mac?" And your answer must come from your vision.

To truly build a business that supports your clients with the value they want in an extraordinary way, create a service that adds value and is unique to you and then name it.

Do you want generic advice on how much to put into your 401(k) so you can retire at age sixty-five? You can get that anywhere. But if a plan or a model that will show you step by step how to get from where you are now to the lifestyle you envision at retirement, you might be able to get that only from the advisor with the unique

11 https://money.usnews.com/money/retirement/articles/most-frequently-asked-retirement-questions

> To scale, you must take your unique approach and turn it into a product. You must answer the question "What is my Big Mac?" And your answer must come from your vision.

name for their plan. It's a proprietary name for the package of services they offer. And it sets them apart in the marketplace.

Here's how you can do the same thing. First, create a proprietary process that represents your vision and the value you can add to your customers. Second, name it. Third, trademark it.

One advisor we work with decided to see how congruent his marketing was with what his office actually offered. He had his team join him in the conference room. Then he drew a big line down the middle of the whiteboard. On the left, he wrote out everything he does for his clients. On the right, he identified how he represents himself and what he does for marketing and messaging.

When he compared the two sides, the disparities were profound. His office was, in essence, underselling what they did and nearly always shortchanging their own narrative. This was a revelation for them. The realization that they had been inadvertently underrepresenting their offerings was both an epiphany and a call to action.

That defining moment—the contrast visible on the whiteboard—became their pivot. It ignited a renewed energy to sculpt a message and a process that truly encapsulated their message and brand, differentiating them from all the others. While advisors often think this process is daunting and they are apprehensive about their own creativity, for this office, it was fun and exciting because they knew that work aligned with their vision.

Dedicating yourself to uncovering your genuine impact and authentic self will be transformative in all aspects of your business. And more often than not, what emerges from this exploration is a renewed sense of purpose and a narrative that genuinely resonates with those you serve.

The Proprietary Process

There are many ways to approach retirement planning. What's yours? Specifically, how do you guide clients through that process? What's unique about your approach? What services do you provide that makes yours different from the competition's? Create your process, map it out clearly, and be sure it has something that distinguishes your particular methodology.

Give Your Process a Name

Retirement Roadmap is a great example of a name, but you can come up with one equally useful. Choose a name that includes the distinctive element you offer. There are plenty of examples of this from all types of businesses. A Whopper is a big hamburger, so big that it takes two hands to hold it. A Full Focus Planner is a daily planning tool, but it does more than list appointments and tasks; it helps you focus on what matters most. Dollar Shave Club isn't just a place to buy men's grooming needs. It's a low-cost subscription service. Choose a name that uniquely identifies your product in the marketplace.

Trademark It

This is a relatively simple process, and it ensures that you and only you can use the name that offers a unique product you've created. A trademark establishes your place in the market, communicates your brand distinction, and improves your brand recognition.

When you create a unique product, you have a base upon which to build your brand message. The product exemplifies your distinctive approach to financial advising and is the ultimate object of your messaging.

Why Congruency Matters

Lead generation and lead conversion are the two main phases of a marketing plan.

Lead generation brings people in contact with your business. That may happen through an email, a seminar invitation, or a word-of-mouth recommendation from a friend. Lead generation is your prospect's first awareness of who you are and what you offer.

Lead conversion, on the other hand, turns those prospects or leads into clients. For a lead to convert, your message to them must be consistent throughout all your marketing and must be congruent with the services you will eventually offer. If there's any mismatch between your lead-generation messaging and what you offer, your marketing will not succeed. To put it another way, the reason people come in contact with your business is the same reason they'll stay with you as a client—your authenticity. If your first message promises one thing and your product promises another, they won't stay around.

I know an advisor whose initial offer to prospects centered on managing their Social Security income. He discussed Social Security strategies that included when to begin drawing the benefit and how to manage the tax liability of the income. Looking at his ads, you could easily conclude that he was offering himself up as an expert on managing Social Security income. Not surprisingly, he got hundreds of leads. Lots of people wanted to know how to get more value from their Social Security checks.

However, this advisor's actual product offer had little to do with Social Security. His core business focused on financial planning. When his sales team met with leads generated by his Social Security messaging, the meetings were a total waste of time. People immediately understood that the real offer had nothing to do with Social Security. Not only did this advisor's marketing lead to a bait and switch, it was totally incongruent with the actual product. His marketing failed to attract the people he actually wanted to serve.

To ensure that your marketing messages align with your product offer, audit your marketing messaging. Look at your initial advertising, your email chains, and text messages. Review the sales copy your advisors use and the language you use in closing. Does it match? If you can spot the incongruency between what you use to draw leads and nurture them versus what you're actually asking those leads to commit to, you'll quickly spot it.

This is a great exercise for getting your marketing messages to align. Alignment doesn't mean that each message must use the exact same verbiage. It means they're all driving to the same end.

When you develop marketing strategies and materials, you must be 100 percent in tune with your audience and their felt

> Alignment doesn't mean that each message must use the exact same verbiage. It means they're all driving to the same end.

needs. All your messages must line up both with your product offer and the perceived need of the target audience.

Congruent marketing forces us to specifically advertise what we're best at so we can attract appropriate clients we are best able to help. Congruent marketing aligns your end point—your product offer—with your starting point, what attracts them to your company in the first place. Congruent messaging places you, your client, your staff, and your product all on the same page.

What It Means to Target

Along with differentiation and congruent messaging, your marketing messages must also target the right audience. That means they should speak directly to your ideal client. For example, if you're best equipped to help people who have $500,000 or more in investable assets, your message must convey that. What you say on the radio and what you offer on a direct mail piece must coincide with the message given to clients when they visit the office. Your team must provide the relevant skills to properly advise $500,000 clients when they come through the door. Remember, marketing is your opportunity to share your authentic vision with the client. It's a chance to show who you are, why you are different, and how you can help.

Many advisors latch onto any message they can think of to attract clients. If the hot topic in the area is Medicare or Medicaid, they tailor their marketing materials and seminars toward Medicare or Medicaid. If their ideal goal is to talk about investments or life insurance, talking about Medicare or Medicaid isn't congruent with what they do. That makes the sales process much more difficult and also frustrates the consumer. It also doesn't get the right prospects in front of advisors, so it's a waste of time. And it's arguably unethical.

Target your messaging toward the people you want to attract. Do not market to fill seats with just anyone. Market to fill seats with the right people, the people you have tailored your product offer around, the people you and your staff have the competence and experience to serve well. There are hundreds of tricky ways to backdoor people into the office, but that's the wrong approach to scaling your business. Fishing with a wide net won't help you create a long-term, sustainable business. Get clear on who you want to serve, what their needs are, and how you can help them. Then target your messaging at those people and those outcomes.

One of our top advisors hosted a seminar that was all about annuities. He was a great annuities professional and felt annuities would benefit his ideal client. His marketing message focused on annuities from start to finish, from the first mailer to the email confirmation to the text message reminders. Can you guess who showed up for the seminar? People who were interested in annuities. During the seminar, he got straight to the point, explaining the advantages of annuities and how they could help the attendees. The seminar produced a good number of appointments, and he closed at a very high rate.

Another advisor I work with focuses on income planning, so that's what he markets. It's income planning in the mailer, income planning at the seminar, and income planning during his meetings. Income planning—that's all he does. People don't talk to him about stocks, Medicaid, or bonds, and he never markets to people who are interested in those things. Prospects come to him for one thing and one thing only—income planning. That's what happens when your marketing messages are differentiated, congruent, and targeted. The marketing aims at your ideal client and connects with their pain points.

Contrary to what you've probably been taught, it's better to have five good prospects at your door than fifty who don't match the profile you're trying to attract. If you're looking for clients with more than $250,000 to invest, your marketing messages must speak to the needs of that audience. The same goes for $100,000 clients or $1 million clients. You cannot tailor a message to the $250,000 investor and expect to get calls from someone looking to invest $1 million.

Think of your marketing messages like the ads that pop up on your social media feed. Have you ever noticed that those ads always relate to your most recent search? If you looked up hiking gear on Google, you'll see dozens of ads for trekking poles, boots, and outdoor clothing. If you search vacation spots, your feed will be jammed with resorts from Cancun to Jamaica. Social media advertisers understand targeted messaging. They don't waste their money putting an ad for a backpack in front of someone who is looking for a luxury cruise. Your marketing strategy must do the same. Focus on your ideal client, and ignore the rest.

One of the advisors I coach targeted his TV ads to potential clients with $100,000 in investable assets. That's exactly who

> Contrary to what you've probably been taught, it's better to have five good prospects at your door than fifty who don't match the profile you're trying to attract.

walked in the door the next week—people looking to invest about $100,000. A week later, he targeted his ads to people with $300,000 in investable assets. Guess what? Those with $300,000 in investable assets came knocking. Targeted messaging really works. But that being said, you should identify your ideal client based on much more than money.

Target markets are also identified by gender, age, and other characteristics. A sixty-year-old man with no family or house payment will respond to a different message than a young couple with three kids and a mortgage. The millionaire next door who no one would ever know had money will have different spending needs than someone who loves cars, boats, and houses. One of my advisors has a lot of small town farmers as clients. He's a great match for them. He knows them, and his desire to help them is authentic to him. Once you identify your ideal client, tailor the message to them, and get that message out through the correct marketing channel. A conservative radio show attracts conservatives. A radio show discussing family values attracts listeners interested in family.

Chapter 11

Transformational Takeaways

- If you don't differentiate yourself from the competition, consumers will compare on price alone, and you'll never scale.
- Differentiate by creating a proprietary process that has a name and is trademarked.
- Your marketing messaging must be congruent so the prospect hears the same thing from the first time they meet you until they become a client.
- Authenticity resonates with consumers—market as who you truly are and what you offer.
- Your message must hit your target market—your ideal client—to be effective.

12

APPROACHING A MARKETING STRATEGY TO SCALE

In this business, it's better to be a chameleon than a pioneer.

— Top advisor

Chapter 12 Transformational Targets

- Decide whether you're building your marketing strategy from proven strategies, innovation, or both.
- Focus on who your marketing efforts bring to your business.
- Throwing money at a marketing tactic without a strategy to support the tactic never works.

I used the metaphor of a slot machine to explain how various advisors approach marketing. Some see it as a typical slot machine that occasionally pays a big jackpot but usually just takes your money. They see marketing as a risk. Others have learned that when marketing is done correctly, it is like a slot machine that always pays out. Naturally, they're eager to feed all the cash they can into that kind of machine.

Here's the point. You can build the kind of slot machine that always pays out. You do that by changing how you approach marketing and then designing a marketing plan that consistently brings new prospective clients to your door. When you build a plan with the right approach and work it consistently, it's like going to Las Vegas and hitting the jackpot every time. There's no risk, only the reward that comes from consistently doing the things that are proven to produce results. The big question is this: How can I build that kind of marketing slot machine?

First, let's look at how to approach marketing. There are two things you need to consider when considering a marketing strategy.

1. Whether you want to model your marketing on proven strategies, innovations, or both
2. How you're going to build your ideas into your business

Deciding to Model or Innovate

There are two approaches to choosing a marketing plan—the modeling approach and the innovation approach.

The Modeling Approach

The modeling approach is the easiest and actually the most predictable of the two plans. Essentially, modeling is finding out what works for others and tailoring it to fit your business. If you really want to find great marketing ideas for your business, you will find many. They're practically everywhere. You can discover them in books, articles, conferences, and industry events. You can find them by having conversations with other advisors or business coaches.

Have you ever heard the saying that goes something like this? When the student is ready, the teacher will appear. It's true. When you are ready to learn about marketing, you'll find more best practices that other advisors are using to successfully market their businesses than you could possibly use. There are literally hundreds of great ways to do it. But you have to look for them with an open mind in order to find them. You can go to a mastermind group or a business conference, or you can just ask a friend or two. If you seek, you will find, and when you find it, you can start modeling. But remember to make sure the strategies that you adopt are consistent with your vision, target audience, and brand.

Yet a word of caution: while modeling after others will be invaluable, it is paramount you don't copy and paste the strategy fully. You must ensure that you stay consistent with your brand and message. Typically, this represents a 10 to 20 percent revision, while the core strategy remains the same.

Based on my experience, I'd say that modeling someone else's successful marketing strategy has a success rate of at least 90 percent, possibly higher. That's because the methodology has been tested and proven. In fact, once a top producer told me, "In this business, it's better to be a chameleon than a pioneer." When you adapt a successful marketing strategy to your business, it will probably work for you too. But you do have to do it right, as we have already discussed.

The Innovation Approach

The second way to build your marketing slot machine is through innovation. Simply put, you can try new things, see if they work, and then improve them or abandon them and try something else. Entrepreneurs often gravitate toward innovation more than they probably should because innovation is risky—much riskier than modeling.

Innovation is different than modeling. My estimate is that the success rate of marketing strategies that advisors create on their own is about 10 percent. There's much less risk in modeling your strategy after best practices, but the idea of creating your own next big idea is always attractive.

Fortunately, there's a place for both approaches. Modeling is the more certain path, but you can always sprinkle in some innovation as well. Just don't risk too much of your budget or time on the innovation side. And when you innovate, be prepared to experience failure—a lot of it. As a general rule, don't put more than 10 percent of your marketing budget into innovative ideas, no matter how great they sound. If you do, then you will be playing with fire, and a bad move could cause devastating consequences to your business.

Even when you are trying and failing (that 10 percent of your budget), remember that marketing works together outside of each individual marketing effort. For example, many of your clients will come to you over time, those who have had several interactions with your marketing efforts. Rarely can they point to one campaign or one medium that brought them in. They'll come in following a campaign or seminar and say, "Bob and Suzie referred us to you, but I also have seen your TV commercials, received your seminar flyer, and heard your radio show." Rarely does someone's first experience with your brand result in contact from a new prospect. But every time they interact with your brand—a flyer, a seminar, word of mouth—it lends credibility to your brand. So marketing works in ways that are not always immediately trackable.

Techniques for Building Marketing into Your Business

Whether you decide to model an existing marketing strategy or innovate your own, finding the ideas is really the easy part. The hard part is building those ideas into your business. Often, people underestimate the amount of thoughtful effort it takes to properly build a marketing strategy that will work for them in the context of their business. To build successfully, you'll need to pay attention to five basic marketing techniques.

1. Prepare for execution
2. Don't expect the money to do the work
3. Get ready to iterate
4. Ignore praise; watch cash flow
5. Avoid the temptation to spend on branding techniques alone

Prepare for Execution

Years ago, an advisor I knew heard that hosting seminars was a great strategy to find new prospects, so he decided to model it. He scheduled the event, paid for a mailer, and hosted the seminar. Even though it was his first time to conduct a workshop of this type, he felt confident. He knew he was as good of an advisor as his peers and figured he would enjoy the same results, maybe even better. He spoke with passion and felt that he crushed it. He was certain that the response cards would flood in with new prospects seeking appointments. But they didn't. The event failed to produce even one appointment. It was an epic bomb.

The advisor left that experience saying, "I'm never doing that again. Seminars just don't work." Of course, that wasn't the case. Seminars were working for many advisors. The problem wasn't the strategy. It was the execution. He had been overconfident about his speaking ability and underprepared for the event. In his arrogance, he didn't pay attention to all the little things that go into making an event work. He did nothing to warm up the prospects before the event, he didn't prepare the room correctly, and he didn't teach his team how to work the event. He dabbled and hoped for the best. That never works.

Unfortunately, you can't just take someone else's strategy and drop it into your business plan with no preparation. Execution is always harder than it looks. What seems like an easy, no-prep tactic almost always requires a good deal of advance planning and attention to detail. Whether you are modeling or innovating, do your homework. Learn the full strategy that makes it successful. Pay attention to the seemingly small factors that can mean the difference between success and failure. If you don't plan to succeed, you plan to fail.

Don't Expect the Money to Do the Work

You have to prepare for execution, but you also can't simply throw money into a strategy and hope the dollars will do the work for you. Recently, I spoke with an advisor who had heard that television advertising was a great marketing strategy for advisors. He knew others who were getting great results from TV spots, so he decided to give it a try. He bought the airtime and showed up to do the segment. Unfortunately, he didn't do the proper due diligence on how to make it work.

Before you purchase airtime, you have to do a ton of due

diligence to make sure your message hits the right people. Then you have to make sure to set yourself up for success when you show up on the show. You have to look great and know the co-host. You have to understand what your core message is, and you have to nail the CTA that is congruent with that message so that it resonates with your audience. Once it's over, you have to have a plan to engage with the leads that come through scripting, proactive and reactive communication, and ongoing drip campaigns.

This advisor just figured, "It's TV. I'll show up and speak, and the results will pour in."

Unfortunately, he learned the hard way that TV doesn't work that way.

As with most marketing, there is an art to making it work, and you've got to go all in to create it right, or a huge investment may end up being a huge mistake. This advisor's mistake cost him $50,000 over a few months, as well as a lot of time and stress. That didn't include the opportunity costs he incurred from not getting the results he could have gotten had he put his time and money elsewhere.

If you have the courage to spend the money on a marketing strategy, take the time to learn how it works. You can't depend on the dollars alone to produce the result. Hone your message, rehearse your performance, get feedback from experts—do everything you can ahead of time to put the odds in your favor. Money can buy a lot of things, but it can't buy execution. You have to build the process to make the strategy successful.

On the other side of this, I've known advisors who have dialed in their process to the 1,000th degree. They know exactly how their team should work a room. They've polished and rehearsed the opening of their presentation, and they know precisely what they want to communicate to the audience and how to do it. In whatever medium—seminars, workshops, video, social media, television—they have dialed in the preparation so well that success is nearly guaranteed. I've seen it time and time again, a well-prepared advisor executing a proven strategy that reaps a tremendous return. As a bonus, the advisor and their team have fun doing it. When your team experiences that kind of success, they'll be dying to repeat it.

Whatever strategy you choose, find out what it takes to make it work. It's never as easy as it looks from the outside, and there will be more details than you realize. Invest the time in learning, crafting, rehearsing, and executing well. Otherwise, you're just flipping a coin and hoping for the best.

Get Ready to Iterate

All marketing strategies carry some risk, even if they've been proven to work for another advisor's business. There are always variables from one context to another. The first time you try something, consider it a test for your market. Don't take too big of a risk on any first-time marketing plan. I'm a big believer in starting small. Risk the least amount possible to gauge the results. Remember the advisor who dropped $50,000 on TV marketing and saw zero return? What if he had initially invested just $5,000 or $10,000?[12] He could have monitored the results, corrected any problems, and tried again. The lessons he could have bought for $5,000 ended up costing $50,000, which was enough to discourage him from investing more.

As you build your marketing machine, consider your initial attempts at any strategy to be a market test. Invest no more than

12 TV spots vary widely in price. What might cost $5,000 in one market, could cost $50,000 in another. The point here is to test before spending all of your money on a new funnel.

you're prepared to lose. Then debrief the experience with your team.

- What worked? What didn't? Why?
- How can you address these problems next time around?
- How can you maximize the things that worked well?

Remember, as the leader, it's up to you to own the results. Avoid blaming the team for a failure. Be the first to speak up about any mistakes you may have made. That will create an atmosphere where others feel free to share their ideas. You need that if you're going to get better results the next time around.

Ignore Praise; Watch Cash Flow

When it comes to marketing, the general rule is that Outflow = Inflow = Cash Flow. That means the more you invest in marketing, the more new clients you will develop, and the more revenue you'll receive. That's what should happen when you invest in marketing.

That should be obvious, but it isn't always. Very often, advisors evaluate only the "outflow" part of the equation. In other words, they look at their marketing efforts and are taken in by how professional, slick, or inviting they appear. In reality, they're seeing fool's gold. Their plan looks effective, and that makes them feel good. But it may not be producing the result they're after.

Here's an example. Let's say you do an appearance on a radio or TV show. The experience is kind of fun, and you imagine that you're getting fantastic exposure for your business. A day or two later, you go to church, and a friend approaches you. "Hey, I saw you on TV this week. That was awesome. Great job!" Obviously, that affirmation feels good. It may even trick you into thinking your marketing plan is working. After all, people are watching you! Now you have someone telling you how great it was or how wonderful you looked. It's an easy conclusion to make. But is it a valid conclusion? Not necessarily.

First, your friend was excited to see someone they knew on television. Naturally, they're going to be excited about it. And even if it wasn't a stellar performance, your buddy or girlfriend isn't going to tell you that during a casual encounter. Friends are generally unreliable witnesses when it comes to giving feedback unless you specifically ask them for an honest critique. Even then, they're likely to give only positive feedback.

Second, we are all more prone to look for evidence that we are right than evidence that we are wrong. Psychological researchers have developed a term for this. It's called confirmation bias. When evaluating yourself or your efforts, you're naturally inclined to amplify the evidence that confirms your success while ignoring evidence that proves you wrong. So you hope and believe that your TV strategy will work, and your friend confirms that belief. But that doesn't make it so.

Remember the formula Outflow = Inflow = Cash Flow. The core measure of success in marketing is whether it gets results. That makes it vital that you learn to filter out the other signals and monitor your numbers to determine whether your investment was worthwhile. The ROI for marketing dollars is not congratulations from friends or even clients who say they liked whatever that effort was. It's cash flowing into the business, proof that it got the results needed for the money you invested. Keep your eye on what matters most. If your marketing is on brand you will also get the benefit of lifting up your brand with all the marketing you are doing.

Avoid the Temptation to Spend on Branding Techniques Alone

One marketing pitfall for advisors is placing a disproportionate emphasis on branding without a broader marketing strategy. Consider this formula: your marketing outflow should be directly proportional to the inflow of customers, resulting in cash flow (Outflow = Inflow = Cash Flow). Again, this is the equation or code in order to scale your marketing.

As we discussed, your brand is integral to this. It sets the tone for all your marketing efforts and consistently reinforces your message. As you build your brand, your marketing should concurrently yield tangible results, allowing you to continue investing. A well-established brand can indeed amplify the success of all marketing endeavors, especially if it underscores your distinctiveness. So while branding is essential, the majority of your marketing budget should translate to a direct return on investment.

Building a recognizable brand is a marathon, not a sprint. It comprises numerous small, consistent efforts over time. Conversely, effective marketing can and should yield quicker results. To truly scale, both need to work in tandem, optimizing your budget and

Building a recognizable brand is a marathon, not a sprint. It comprises numerous small, consistent efforts over time.

getting the most out of your dollars.

Let's consider a real-life example. In the past, I visited with a successful advisor, Randy, who noticed his profit margin lagging quite a bit behind his peers. His profit margin was around 25 percent while many others were boasting around 35 percent. He couldn't understand how his could be so much less, so we decided to audit his finances and try to find the source of the problem. After half an hour or so of really digging in, a particular line item labeled "billboards" piqued my interest. Upon inquiry, Randy admitted that he couldn't directly trace any new client acquisitions to these billboards, but he relished the brand recognition they offered despite their cost, which matched precisely the 10 percent profit disparity. This anecdote underscores the peril of prioritizing vanity metrics and noise over direct results.

While branding is a luxury that might seem attractive, for most small businesses, it can prove prohibitively costly without immediate returns. It's imperative that your marketing dollar yields results and facilitates sustained business growth. Enter direct response marketing, a strategy that reaches out directly to potential clients, getting a direct response. Done right, this strategy not only gets immediate results but also enhances brand recognition organically.

A well-defined brand will magnetize the right audience, distinctly conveying your identity and offering. All marketing efforts, if coherent, amplify your brand's reach. In Randy's scenario, billboards might have been justifiable if they had been more cost-effective. However, it bled his marketing budget, stunting his business's growth and decreasing his profit as well.

Investing in direct response marketing isn't one size fits all.

Some approaches, like television or radio, cater to a broad audience, while others such as email campaigns target a niche. Tailor your strategy to your budget, and scale as your business expands. Whether you're reaching 10,000 via emails or 100,000 through a TV ad, align your expenses with the outreach. A broader reach demands a bigger budget.

Consistency and adaptability in marketing are paramount. By closely monitoring cash flow and ROI, you can discern when to diversify and upscale. Stay committed, adapt based on results, and incrementally introduce new strategies. This consistency not only maximizes ROI but also propels your business growth.

Chapter 12
Transformational Takeaways

- When you approach your marketing strategy, ask yourself two questions:
  1. Do I want to model my marketing on proven strategies, innovations, or both?
  2. How am I going to build my ideas into my business?
- The modeling approach takes what others are already doing and adapts it to your business. The innovation approach applies new ideas to your strategy.
- An idea without a clear plan for execution never works.
- You can't throw money at a marketing idea and expect it to work without your oversight, intention, and reverse engineering.
- Pay attention to who your marketing efforts are bringing to you, not who within your own circle thinks they're great.
- Don't focus on brand awareness only. Focus on direct response marketing so you get the right people in front of you every time.

Looking to set your marketing mindset for scale? Check out additional resources here.

SECTION 6

SALES

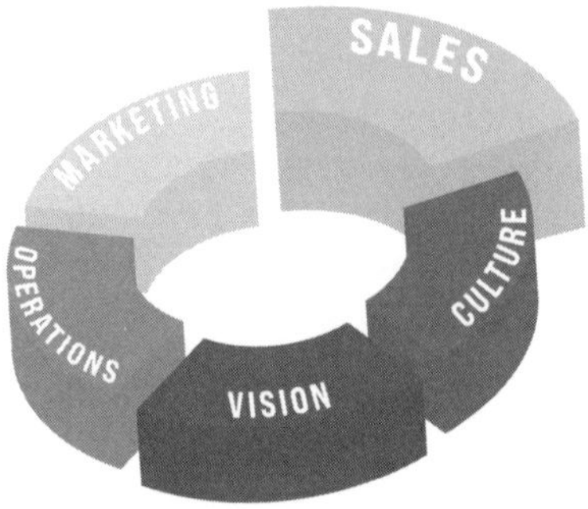

Sales aren't about manipulation or employing sly tactics. They're about making a difference and authentically transferring the belief that you can help someone. If you truly believe you can make a difference for someone, your ability to transfer that belief constitutes the sales process. As you scale your business and it gets better and better, your business should ultimately improve the experience and value you provide your customers. As this happens, the sales process should become much easier since the value is greater and your belief is even more certain that you can help them. However, as straightforward as this sounds, to scale your sales, the odds are stacked against you.

To scale, your process must be duplicatable and trainable. You have to be able to bring in other salespeople and, with a high probability, set them up for success. Over time your business will become less and less dependent on you to bring in revenue. However, as we've mentioned before, industry studies show that more than 70 percent of rookie advisors fail[13]. Some of them quit. Some find that the industry isn't right for them. Others simply don't have what it takes to succeed—so scaling won't be easy. You've got to beat the odds, but it can be done.

13 https://www.barrons.com/advisor/articles/financial-advisor-talent-shortage-cerulli-69010ca9#:~:text=Although%2018%2C207%20new%20trainees%20entered,2%2C459%20advisors%20retired%20in%20 2022.

In Chapter 4, we talked about Anthony and how his team's overall production outpaced his once he got on the Green Line. We shared how production was dependent on him at the beginning of his scaling efforts and what it was like at the end. We showed his progression over five years.

Actual Case Study: The Change in Production and Who Was Responsible for That Production

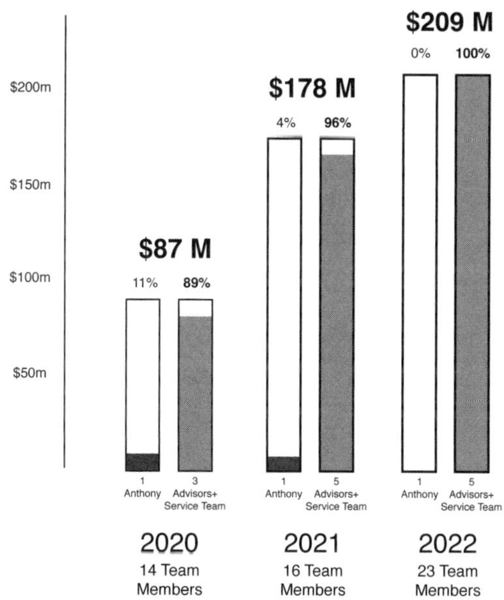

This is what happens when an advisor goes from the Red Line of Success to the Green Line of Significance™. In 2018, Anthony was bringing in $78 million in new assets. No matter what, he would not have been able to triple his production by keeping things the same. He simply didn't have the capacity. However, in three years, business more than doubled and Anthony was responsible for very little of the production. The next year, Anthony's business became fully dependent on the team to make the sales, and Anthony only contributed 4 percent of the total revenue. The design allowed his business to be less dependent on the founder while tripling production at the same time.

The building blocks of a successful, scalable sales business start with the value you can ultimately provide your customers. They also starts with a strong belief and confidence, a clearly designed and duplicatable process, effective training, and a vision that resonates with your clients. Remember, your clients aren't just buying a product or service—they're buying into your mission and your vision. It's your job to make sure they see that value in everything you do.

In the next chapter, we will talk about how to:

- Build a successful sales team that will prepare you for scale.
- Duplicate your sales process.
- Tie your sales process and products to your vision and mission.

Are you ready for your next step toward unlimited growth, freedom, and joy?

13

CREATE A SALES PROCESS THAT SCALES

As an advisor, a scalable sales process is the key to unlimited growth.

— Top advisor

Chapter 13 Transformational Targets

- Create a selling structure that includes selling, planning, and service advisors.
- To scale, develop a three-tiered sales business.
- Create a consistent selling and training process for your team.

Scaling in sales entails the strategic enhancement of your sales team and processes in order to more effectively and efficiently manage increased demand. It results in a higher success rate, increased revenue, and an improved client experience.

When an advisor starts in this business, they have lots of time but little production. However, as they acquire more clients who trust and confide in them, they feel obligated to fulfill their duty to these clients, leaving little time to onboard new ones. This shift transforms their identity from a proactive advisor focused on acquiring new clients—a thrill for most great advisors—to a reactive service person. Overcoming this transformation is crucial to scale.

Understanding the problem's root cause is the first step toward a solution. Most advisors start as a one-person show, selling themselves because they don't have a substantial team. They emphasize their personal contributions, which leads clients to buy into the individual rather than the service. This expectation hinders scaling and often results in burnout and a glass ceiling in terms of production.

Recognizing this issue, many advisors logically conclude, "I need more advisors." They believe growing wide by hiring more advisors will create scale.

So there is really a flaw in the design. What got us here, won't get us there. How do you scale your sales?

The truth is that the sales business is comprised of three different types of advisors, all working together as one team to scale:

- The selling advisor
- The planning advisor
- The service advisor

I believe that one reason the failure rate is so high in this business is that advisors who are hiring always look for all three of these advisors in one. The reality is that some of the skill sets needed for one contradict those needed for another. That is why you need to build a sales team that has a variety of skillsets.

Understand the Individuals on the Sales Team

The sales advisor role generates the highest revenue but also has the highest failure rate. It requires a high skill level to convince clients to trust you with their life savings. This skill level is significantly higher than what is required for a administrative person, whose training may take a day compared to years for an advisor. The industry has incorrectly taught us to seek individuals who have financial knowledge and are relationship-oriented, good planners, analytical, great communicators, and confident. However, it's rare to find all these attributes in one person.

For example, a friend of mine—a CPA and highly analytical individual—excelled at piecing together plans but struggled to close deals with clients. On the other hand, another advisor, a gifted communicator, inspired trust quickly but disliked routine service calls. Another associate was excellent at nurturing relationships but dreaded sales meetings.

Expecting advisors to excel in all areas is a key reason for the high failure rate. Productivity is usually based on sales, so trying to make an analytical person a salesperson, or vice versa, is challenging. Instead of forcing individuals into roles that don't suit them, the Triad Advisory Model™ suggests hiring and training specialists for each role. It involves having a dedicated planner, a salesperson, and a relationship manager, all working together to provide the best overall client experience. To scale your sales team, you need a three-tiered sales business that hires for selling, planning, and service advisor positions that specialize over time.

Avoid Putting People in Roles They Dislike

Many of our best salespeople eventually become full-time service people. Instead of replacing them and trying to find another salesperson, why not optimize your best salesperson's time so they do more sales and less service? You will avoid putting them in a role they won't like. Which role is more likely to succeed, and which one is easier to hire for? This path will increase your probability of success, and you won't be trying to replace yourself in a position that has a high failure rate.

When we suggest this, we often hear, "I can't have a service advisor take over. My clients bought me."

Why is this the case? When you onboard clients correctly, this concern dissipates. We'll discuss this in more detail later in the chapter.

Almost every advisor is expected to become a sales advisor. That's the end of what they were taught for their desired career path. This expectation is incredibly tough. Some advisors don't have the skillset or desire for this role and would be much better off and happier as a long-term planning or service advisor.

Why not create fulfilling career paths where each of these three types advisors can specialize in what they do best and enjoy? This approach is not only best for the business, but it's also best for the individual advisors.

Imagine the Chicago Bulls of the 1990s. If every player wanted to be and was expected to be Michael Jordan—MJ—they wouldn't have won the championships. They'd have an identity crisis that would cause conflict and certainly lose games. Great teams are made up of individuals with different skills and desires. So why in this business do we expect every advisor to do—and enjoy doing—all skillsets?

Let's look at the big picture of what happens when people are put in the wrong positions.

1. They become dissatisfied with their job, leading to decreased productivity and motivation.
2. The money invested in them may be wasted. They may quit to go do something that better uses their skills and increases their productivity.
3. It impacts the culture. A teammate may not only become less engaged with other teammates but may also speak negatively to others about the company and their job.

This situation doesn't work for anyone—not the teammates, not you, not the company, and certainly not your clients.

A great team that works well together is required in order to scale. So how do you set this up? How do you pay each of the three advisors so they are all aligned and fulfilled? You create a three-tiered sales business.

Creating a Three-Tiered Sales Business

A three-tiered sales business develops over time, not when there are just three of you in the office and everyone is doing everything. This is a business of progression, and when you move out of startup mode and into scale, you must create a sales business that focuses on three specialist roles—the selling advisor, the planning advisor, and the service advisor.

Selling Advisors

Selling advisors should be experts at transferring belief to prospects and thrive when promoting and selling your company and process.

As the company's initial contact with the prospect, they get to know the client, understand their needs, and demonstrate how the company can best help them.

Selling advisors have to be great with people. They need to be relationship oriented because their first job is to establish trust, which can't be done if they're not good with people. Since even the best salespeople have a high failure rate, it's critical that your selling advisor can fail, get up quickly, and not let the negative emotions from one contact affect their next one.

Planning Advisors

Planning advisors rely on the groundwork laid by the selling advisor. They conduct in-depth financial assessments of the client's current situation, including income, expenses, assets, and liabilities. Based on that, they create a financial plan for the clients and adjust it over time as needed.

Planning advisors are analytical and love spreadsheets and details. When a planning advisor is put in a selling advisor's role, they often end up confusing everyone. That friend I mentioned earlier—the CPA who tried to become a selling advisor—got way too far into the weeds about everything. In fact, we joked that he would answer complexity with more complexity. As you can imagine, that didn't work. It confused everyone and did a disservice to the clients and the business. Imagine if this person had been hired as a planning advisor. They would have excelled.

The Service Advisor

Rockstar service advisors feed your marketing team with referrals. When someone genuinely takes the time to check on their clients and nurture them through their entire life cycle with the company, that person becomes an abundant referral resource. All this person focuses on is caring for their clients. They send gifts, check in regularly, and invite their families to events. They'll do the things you'd love to do for your clients but don't have the time.

Service advisors are good with people. They are relationship-oriented and have hearts of gold, which is why they are so influential. They are easy to relate to and authentic. People trust them instantly. They're very social and would not thrive if they were stuck analyzing financial plans all day.

These people are on a mission to make a difference and help people, and clients can tell. Usually, when I ask advisors what skillset their advisors need, they combine the skills for all three of these roles. But someone who is great with people isn't always great with details, and vice versa. Someone who loves spreadsheets doesn't necessarily want to spend time caring for clients. To scale your business, you have to hire advisor specialists with the skills for their specific roles.

The three-tiered sales business model leads to less staff turnover, a better culture, and improved productivity.

The three-tiered sales business model leads to less staff turnover, a better culture, and improved productivity. From the client's perspective, it's a huge win. By having each advisor specialize in what they do best, it's a better outcome for clients. This design, as great as it sounds, has an additional benefit as well.

Creating Alignment

Moving away from the one-size-fits-all advisor approach means you'll need to create some alignment with your team and your clients. Rather than viewing the sales team as one salesperson, look at the team as a very carefully coordinated group that works together harmoniously.

Now, how do we create alignment?

First, your team is all advisors. They just specialize in different areas. No advisor is superior to another, and there aren't any "sub" advisors. This is a very carefully crafted team of experts. The entire team has to understand the model and why it's in place, including how they will all benefit from this design.

In the sales process, your selling advisors must "sell the team," not themselves. Imagine a twenty-three-year-old advisor sitting down with a sixty-five-year-old man, trying to convince him to manage his $1 million in assets. It won't happen. But imagine this young advisor selling the team and how the team will manage his money. The team is much more validated than the individual. Clients don't want a "guy" or a "gal"; they want a great team to help them. This increases validation and removes the long-term stress on one person's time. It leans on the bandwidth of the team as a whole. This scales. A nice offset of this is that selling the team also relieves the pressure on the young person who no longer has to sell their limited experience.

Selling your team starts with the selling advisor and never ends. It continues through the entire life cycle of your client's experience with your business. So whenever there's an opportunity, sell your team. For example, one of our offices has a picture of their whole team in each conference room. During their process, they point out the picture and really highlight the fact that they have a great team to help.

Finally, the sales process needs to carefully incorporate each team member seamlessly. Let me paint a picture for you.

A sales advisor runs the first meeting and asks all the discovery questions as per usual. But in the sales meeting is the service advisor is riding shotgun. The salesperson builds up the other advisor, emphasizing that they work as a team. As soon as the meeting is over, the service advisor dictates the notes from the meeting, which go directly to the planner who then starts putting together the plan. The service advisor then sends a recap to the client. Notice that the sales advisor does not. That establishes a clear expectation with that person. Before the next meeting, the sales advisor reviews the plan, making sure it's exactly what they need. Then they meet with the client and go over the planning. When the client is onboarded, the service advisor once again rides shotgun and recaps the meeting. The service advisor calls the client post-meeting to keep them updated on how it's all going.

Typically, the sales advisor is commission-based. The service and planning advisors tend to get nice salaries and have bonuses based on the team's success. The service advisor also gets an incentive for any referrals or additional business they uncover, and then they bring the sales advisor back to help.

You may be wondering about specific compensation numbers.

Unfortunately, that is highly situational, and your exact scenario will need to be reviewed in order to get that right. But this design as a whole will increase the ability for you to scale, increase the client experience, and lead to high revenue and margins if done correctly.

3 Ways to Scale

When considering the scaling of your sales process, it's important to understand that there are three main ways to scale your sales team—go wide, bring on larger clients, or generate more revenue per client.

Go wide: This means increasing the number of transactions over time. Instead of bringing on 100 new clients this year, you could aim to double that and bring on 200. That is known as scaling wide or broad.

Bring on larger clients: Rather than acquiring 100 clients with $500,000 each in assets, you could target clients with $1 million or $1.5 million in assets, thereby doing two to three times the volume with the same number of clients.

Generate more revenue per client: This can be achieved by adding more services to each client so they do more business with you and less elsewhere.

As you consider the three ways to scale sales, remember that a scalable model as a whole like we've discussed will ultimately allow you to grow in all three dimensions. Think about your sales process. Rather than having your salesperson be the bottleneck, you can adopt a team approach that allows you to focus more time on sales meetings with your best people.

The better you build your business, the more valuable it will become. High-net-worth individuals will join a team in a situation where they wouldn't have joined an individual advisor because that person doesn't have the team or process to bring them on. That will increase your average case size, and you will be able to capture all their money rather than just a little here and there. They are buying your full team and process, not just a commodity product.

> The better you build your business, the more valuable it will become.

Finally, advisors can incorporate comprehensive financial planning for their clients. You really can't do thorough financial planning without understanding the client's goals, what they have, and what they need. We've found that our advisors who do this right will secure the safe money, investments, and life insurance for estate planning as well. All these are needs within the plan to fulfill, which is what the clients joined them for.

Become a Dynamic Steppingstone

Once you've learned how to scale and started building a three-tiered sales business, you can rock the client experience. In the high-speed, distraction-riddled world of sales, maintaining momentum is pivotal. Each meeting you have—every conversation you conduct with a prospective client who needs your help—forms an essential steppingstone that leads to the next. This sequential, continuous movement is one of the most critical things about an effective sales process.

Consider this. You've just wrapped up a highly productive, emotional meeting. The energy is a perfect ten. However, if you allow two to three weeks to elapse before the next meeting, the impact you made in that meeting begins to wane, slowly but surely.

As each day passes, the emotional resonance of your interaction diminishes, fading into the backdrop of your client's busy life. By the time your next meeting rolls around, the once-vivid recollections of the previous session become hazy at best. As a result, a significant portion of your next meeting will be spent recapturing the essence of the initial encounter, hoping you both gain the same clarity you had in the prior meeting so you can take the next step. To ensure forward motion, this cycle of refresh and repeat needs to be minimized. You need to maintain momentum so you can best help them when it is top of mind, and they can take the next step as well.

1. Execute Your Appointment Cadence with Intentional, Strategic Fluidity

A seamless progression of meetings ideally spaced no more than a week apart should be your goal. With this rhythm, each appointment cascades into the next, keeping the dialogue fresh and top-of-mind for you both.

To see how important this is, underscore at the end of each meeting the importance of this rhythm. Initiate a conversation about the seriousness of the client's commitment to the issue at hand, reinforcing the client's need for clarity or resolution to prioritize the steps in the process. Make it clear that given the rapid pace of life and the noisy world we live in, the process works best if you don't space the meetings too far apart, which risks diminishing the impact, forcing you to somewhat repeat much of the steps as opposed to moving forward in the process built to help them.

When meetings occur in quick succession, the process remains dynamic, fresh, and compelling. Once a client acknowledges the logic in this, propose your next meeting for the following week and ask if they can make that work. The key here is securing the client's agreement and commitment right then with a real understanding of why that's necessary. This won't be perfect, but if nothing else, it will decrease the time between steps versus leaving it wide open. So if it's not the next week, it will typically shorten the cycle regardless.

2. Begin by Anchoring Back to the Key Points Discussed in the Previous Session

This enables a swift recalibration and reengagement with the issues that matter most. It will quickly get your client back to that feeling they had when they left the last meeting, which then allows you to carry on with the next step in the process.

Open with a recap of the needs and concerns they had, the possible solutions you discussed, and any insights gained. Then invite them to share any questions or additional insights they might have had in the interim. This dialogue reinforces their engagement in the process, validates their involvement, and sets the stage for the meeting so all parties can move forward.

3. Remember That You Are Human

Your brain is flawed, and your memory over time will fade. You will pick up critical information from your clients in these conversations, and you will lose some of that information as your mind competes with life and everything that comes with it. Whether it's other meetings, family—whatever it is—it is critical that you take great notes. These notes should include any important information you gain—the concerns, the meaning to them, the emotions or triggers that they may have shared, and the expectations they had and you had. Each point should be documented, and that document should provide you with a full recap you can use prior to the next meeting so it puts your mind in the same place it was in the last meeting.

By implementing these strategies, you transform each meeting from a static interaction into a dynamic steppingstone. Momentum builds, progress accelerates, and the path to successful sales becomes clearer, shorter, and more effective. This is the secret to crafting a compelling, momentum-driven sales journey.

How Great Sales Teams Lead to Referrals

We'll talk more about culture a little bit later, but when your advisors are doing what they love and you've created a three-tiered sales structure that works for them, the business, and the clients, it creates a great culture, and great cultures build referral-based businesses.

For example, one of our offices brings in $300 million a year. They manage over $1 billion, and they have completely adopted this three-tiered sales team design. Their business is a well-oiled machine. They have a team of great service advisors, planners, and salespeople. Because of this, more than $100 million a year comes from referrals.

The key? They've created an incredible client experience that no one else can touch. Today, their service advisors are their key relationship people. Their clients know and trust them and enjoy their interactions with them. In the past, when the sales advisor had to stop what they were doing to take care of a client, they were super mission focused, got it done quickly, and then move on to what they love—bringing in clients. Today, however, the service team meets with a client when they need something—this is their core job—and takes the extra time to go above and beyond with the relationship. Yes, the client's needs will be taken care of just like they were with the selling advisor. But guess what? The service advisor also stops to ask, "How's your new grand baby?"

This office has found that service advisors are incredible at generating referrals. They go into conversations and then in the end learn that a client's neighbor was asking about who they use. An introduction is made, and there you go. Because the service advisor is compensated based on the referrals and repeat business they get, they also have incentive to continue this cycle.

As you know, the highest profit business they get is referrals. There isn't much cost at all, especially compared to the marketing costs we covered in the marketing section. The three-tiered sales business can help you get them.

In my first book, The Advisor Breakthrough, I said—boldly—that if you're not getting referrals, you probably don't deserve them. I still believe this.

How many referrals you get directly correlates to how much value you bring to your clients. If you've got service advisors who are just crushing it, that adds value. If you have shown time and time again that you provide value that other firms don't, you'll get referrals. If you show up like everyone else, there's nothing special about you. You must go above and beyond all client expectations if you're looking to build a referral-based business. Your team must also be committed to creating a referral-based business.

The Elephant in the Room: What If My Advisors Leave?

We all know that finding good advisors is challenging. So what if you follow these suggestions, find some great selling, planning, and service advisors, and then, instead of having them close deals and service customers while you're on vacation, they leave and become competitors? Unfortunately, such limiting beliefs prevent us from scaling because they don't ask the question, "How can I make my business so good for them, that they never want to leave?" When you don't have a training program that truly supports these advisors and helps them become part of your well-thought-out brand and processes, advisors will either fail or leave.

Most advisory businesses are not structured for scaling or ready for additional advisors. They bring on new advisors, expect them to have the skills and interest in all three advisory roles, view them as mentees, and fail to give them any streamlined process to work from. Too often, these advisors not only become disgruntled, but because they handle their marketing, operations, and processes like they would on their own, they leave. Essentially, they become independent operators working within someone else's business, which is a suboptimal design for a fraction of the revenue.

Conversely, imagine a company where the advisor gains higher net worth clients due to the brand and proprietary process. Picture an advisor with a calendar full of appointments, doing what they love while all operations, planning, and service tasks are handled for them. Their sole responsibility is doing what they love, and that will enable them to do more business with the company than they could independently, and without the headaches.

This scenario is made possible with a comprehensive training process that inverts the odds of success, making it easier to get up and running, and fostering loyalty. It also hinges on a fair deal between both parties, one where the business gains a great advisor and the advisor sees more potential and certainty with the company than independently.

Triad's top three offices have multiple advisors generating revenue and not a single one of them has left. That's zero turnover. Do you see the difference?

Chapter 13 Transformational Takeaways

- No one advisor is the same. They each offer different skillsets and interests, which is why you need to hire selling, planning, and service advisors.
- Forcing people such as service advisors into roles they don't enjoy leads to job dissatisfaction, decreased productivity, and negative cultural side effects.
- Creating a three-tiered sales business will allow the sales side of your business to scale.
- Consistency in how you treat and train your team is critical to scale.

14

THE KEYS TO SCALING SALES

You have no idea how much confidence I have going into a meeting knowing that all I have to do is follow the process that you laid out for me. That's why I succeed.

— Top advisor

Chapter 14 Transformational Targets

- First and foremost, create a sales team that believes in you and your vision.
- Create congruent sales and marketing processes to instill confidence in your clients.
- Ensure every one of your advisors knows your sales process inside and out.

Sales are all about transferring belief. That's not just true for salespeople. It's true for business owners. If you want to hire and keep good advisors, you must transfer to them the belief, mission, and vision that you have for your company before they can transfer the same to anyone else. Your job is to make your company so valuable that your advisors will never leave.

Sales are all about transferring belief. That's not just true for salespeople. It's true for business owners.

When you create an incredible process and then train your team how to successfully use that process, you create downstream opportunities for any advisors who join your team.

Let's return to the McDonald's example. Remember how their process was so successful that even a sixteen-year-old kid without any work experience and not much life experience could walk in, spend a day training, and then work on their own the very next day? The best part is that this short turnaround of training doesn't have any negative impact on the quality of the product and the experience the customers expect from McDonald's. You can do the same with your advisors if you create a good sales process for them to follow.

Build a sales organization that scales by creating an incredible process that is:

- Congruent
- Tangible
- Duplicatable

How to Make Your Process Congruent

One of the most crucial aspects of the sales process is maintaining congruence with your company's identity and messaging. When you bring clients in for the right reasons and deliver what you promise, they naturally become advocates for your business. When the client experiences a lack of congruency, it will feel like a bait-and-switch casualty.

This all comes down to your vision and your mission, which are the heart of your business.

Whatever your vision is, whatever you do, how you can help, and what makes you different must have follow-through.

Congruency in sales means the language on the front end has to match the deliverables on the back end. Everyone on your sales team must understand that.

If you bring people in for estate planning but your salesperson talks all about income planning, that is a disconnect and will hurt the results. Your initial interaction with the client sets their expectation of what it's like to work with you. At a bare minimum, they must trust that you'll do what you say you will do.

Bring your clients in for the right reasons, and then make sure your process meets the expectations you've set for them.

How to Create a Tangible Process

One Triad member brings in around $300 million in new assets annually. When we asked him about the key to his success, he said, "Having a good process helped, but when we built the back end to deliver on that promise, business really took off."

#DBDL

Delivering on your promise means paying attention to every interaction your client has with not just you but your entire office. What's the experience when they call your office? Does someone answer the phone, or do they get voicemail? If someone answers the phone, are they pleasant and helpful? Do they reflect the promise that you made through your vision and during your first interaction with them?

If you've told prospects that you're going to help them live a worry-free or fearless retirement and the person who answers their calls is either an answering machine (not a person) or someone who can't help them at all, does that alleviate worry and fear or fuel it?

#DBDL

The sales process is more than just the introduction or the first appointment. It encompasses everything before, during, and after the meeting, including your office environment. Pay attention to details, and set your team up for success. Make sure your team dresses in a way that aligns with your core message. Make sure your front office is clean, organized, and professional and puts your prospects at ease when they enter.

When your clients join, send them a welcome kit, thanking them for joining your community. This can't be a pen and a coaster. It needs to be something really thoughtful and high-end that also reinforces your brand and vision. This is the beginning of the onboarding process, a sixty-day period in which you add as much value as you can. Which events does this new client get access to? Oddly enough, many advisors meet clients when the client goes to an educational event, but then once the prospect becomes a client, they don't invite them to any more events. You should not only invite them to additional events once they've decided to work with you but also set a goal to get them to one of those events within the first sixty days of working with you.

In my experience, when a client attends an event—say a lunch and learn—during those first sixty days, they become raving fans and are more likely to refer a friend. Do more than other advisors are doing. You don't want them to say, "Wow! My current advisor only invites me to one check-in every year."

Developing a tangible process means constantly asking yourself this: How can we improve our client experience? Does it mirror the caliber of work we want to deliver?

I worked with an attorney who meticulously crafted a personalized estate plan for someone who I was working with. The plan was detailed and comprehensive, yet when it came time to hand over the documents, they were presented in a plain manila envelope. That presentation did not reflect the exceptional quality of the attorney's work.

What we deliver to our clients must mirror the high standard of our work. I once heard an advisor say, "Anything a client sees needs to look like a million dollars." This mindset will profoundly influence your sales process. For example, when you confirm an appointment, is it handled professionally? Who makes the call? What tone, style, and message are used?

Every interaction either enhances credibility or seeds doubt. If you give clients a reason to doubt, they will.

Sending a map to your office in the mail is not enough. Instead,

> Every interaction either enhances credibility or seeds doubt. If you give clients a reason to doubt, they will.

imagine sending a copy of your book or a guide about your process, accompanied by a handwritten note expressing your anticipation for the meeting.

The end of the sales process is just the beginning of the client relationship. The sharpest contrast between their previous experience and their new one with you will occur in the first sixty days. What does your onboarding process look like? How many touchpoints do you have?

At Triad, we have a large, plush black chair in each of our main conference rooms. This is our member chair. It's symbolic. We don't let just anyone sit in this chair. It's a constant reminder for everyone on our team to think of the member no matter what they're doing or which decision they're making. When we meet in the room with the chair, we imagine that a member is sitting there with us—in that big black chair—and we keep them fully in mind.

We never stop thinking about the client experience.

How to Create a Process That's Duplicatable

In Section 5, Marketing, we talked about creating a proprietary product that represents your vision. We talked about naming it and then trademarking it. An example would be a plan called the

Retirement Roadmap or a Retirement GPS. This is the product that gives your client buy-in. To get your sales team selling this, you've got to hand them a duplicatable sales process.

This process needs to show how you open the appointment and what you do and say throughout the beginning, middle, and end of it.

The point of this is (1) to create congruency within the client experience and (2) to give the sales team more confidence. The more confident they are, the more likely they are to stay. The happier they are, the more likely they are to increase productivity and provide excellent service to your clients.

SCALE

During this process, avoid giving your new sales team member too much information. Just like the economics professor I mentioned earlier, if you try to share your thirty years of experience with someone who just started, they will quickly become overwhelmed and as a result become discouraged. This new hire does not need to know it all. They can't possibly learn everything you've experienced throughout your career in a quick window of time. What they need is a PhD in your process only.

To scale, you've got to have a clear, step-by-step process that clients go through. You then have to break that process down into a curriculum so new advisors have something to work from while they move through new situations and experiences with clients. You can't speed up real-life experience no matter how many meetings the new advisor attends. So while they're learning through on-the-job experience, give them the training they need to follow a process so they have confidence that if they follow the process, it will work.

One of the advisors I work with did this, and within one year,

> They can't possibly learn everything you've experienced throughout your career in a quick window of time. What they need is a PhD in your process only.

the twenty-three-year-old that he hired closed $30 million in new assets. This kid told my advisor, "You have no idea how much confidence I have going into a meeting knowing that all I have to do is follow the process that you laid out for me. That's why I succeed." Do you see the impact that curriculum training can have on your new hires—and on your bottom line?

This advisor's process and curriculum were so dialed in that he did for his office what McDonald's did for its process. You can do the same.

Finally, to scale sales, you need to take a four-tiered approach to your process.

The Four-Tiered Approach to Unlocking Sales at Scale

1. Product Mastery

Many advisors start their career as a product salesperson. Many may start out by just being a life insurance salesperson. Or they may focus on mutual funds, ETFs, stocks, bonds, or annuities.

Four-Tiered Approach to Unlocking Sales at Scale

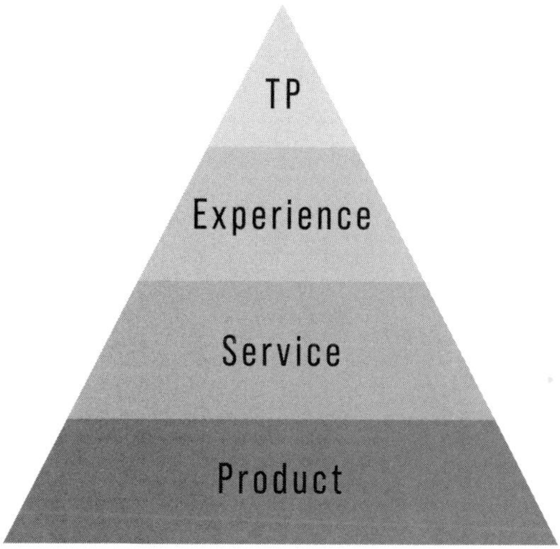

During this phase of selling, the salesperson's aim is to distinguish themselves as an expert in a product, a "buy it from me, I know it better" mentality. They may evolve into being able to sell numerous product offerings and help the client buy several products that will work harmoniously together. But beware! The battleground is fierce at this stage of selling. Regardless of what the salesperson says, each one of them is selling a commodity. And in the world of commodities, price tends to be a determining factor in who to buy from.

Think about it. If you were to buy a new car and the same car was being sold in Lot A and Lot B, but Lot B was selling it for $1,000 less, it doesn't matter how much you like the Lot A owner, you will most likely buy from Lot B because of price.

2. Supreme Service

In order to differentiate their product, salespeople often offer a superior service. They say, "You can get this product from me or the guy down the street, but I will also do XYZ to help you." This, they hope, will set them apart from everyone else who is selling the same commodity. This is a step ahead. As we mentioned, it's no surprise that many advisors claim their number-one differentiator is "great service." They think that by offering great service they're differentiating themselves from the competition when in reality they're offering "great service" just like everyone else.

This dimension goes beyond product expertise and delves into a realm where exceptional client service sets you apart. It involves a proactive approach where responsiveness and clear communication become your hallmark. Picture a store where not only are the prices competitive but the customer service is unparalleled. It goes beyond "great service" and instead creates a sanctuary of assistance and guidance for clients. A greeter stands at the front, someone walks around the store with you, if needed, to help you find whatever you need, they bag your groceries, and then somebody brings them to the car for you. It's the same product, the same commodity, but service is excellent, not just good.

3. Exhilarating Experience

Next, we venture into the exhilarating territory of client experiences. In this sphere, you're not just a financial advisor offering products and great service. You're also going above and beyond to create an experience for clients.

I've seen advisors do monthly lunch and learns to help educate clients about what's going on and how additional products might fit into the mix. I've seen client appreciation events that clients love and look forward to—movies, summer BBQs, and more. The products are great, the service is incredible, but the experience is second to none. It does pay off.

4. Transformational Planning

At the pinnacle of our design lies a completely different sale altogether.

It's not selling products, but rather selling a full planning process where salespeople actively partner with clients to meet their planning needs. The goal is to provide a transformational relationship for them to live their best retirement. This is transformational planning.

Transformational planning is a seismic shift from a product-centered approach to one that revolves around meticulous, comprehensive planning. This approach values depth over speed, focusing on cultivating a profound impact through an extended, enriching, ongoing engagement with the client.

Here, we embrace a dynamic blueprint that addresses the five critical pillars of financial planning:

- Income planning
- Investment strategy
- Tax optimization
- Health care preparation
- Legacy planning

This blueprint includes a series of engaging meetings in which each session builds upon the last, weaving a rich tapestry of financial strategies that encompass every facet of your client's life. This approach closes the loop, offering a comprehensive plan that evolves with time and changing circumstances, transforming each interaction into a strategy or development session. Do you see how different this process is to a normal advisor process?

Everyone spends a different amount of time on their sales process. Some believe in moving through the sales process in the shortest amount of time to make the biggest impact. While one meeting might work to sell a product, walking a client through an entire planning process might take four meetings. However long you spend on appointments, always consider how much time will make the best impact, and then choose that option.

Revolutionizing Sales through Transformational Planning

By steering clear of the commodity lane and entering the realm of transformational planning, you redefine your market position. Think of it as the difference between a routine checkup and a complete physical at the Mayo Clinic. Offer your clients an in-depth, thorough analysis that mirrors their serious commitment to safeguarding their retirement. This paradigm shift not only elevates your value but significantly expands your market share.

As we discussed in Chapter 13 when we mentioned the three ways to scale, this process allows you to grow with all three components while increasing the value you bring to your clients. This leads to maximizing transactions, securing larger deals, and boosting margin per deal. By presenting a holistic suite of services, you captivate clients and encourage them to entrust you with their complete portfolio thereby increasing the value derived from each one.

In this transformative journey, the focus shifts from mere products to a planning-centered approach, creating a magnet that attracts more transactions, larger deals, and higher margins. By addressing the specific needs of clients with a comprehensive range of services, you cultivate an environment where every client feels valued and fully catered to. And by selling a process, you aren't doing a quick meeting and calling it a day. Clients are buying into each step of the process one after the other. You don't have to ask for another meeting. The client knows on the front end to expect the next meeting, and the next, and so on.

The transformative planning process is your golden ticket to ascending the heights of the advisory world. It's a beacon that distinguishes you from your competitors, allowing you to carve a niche that is both rewarding and profoundly impactful. Embrace this approach, and watch as your sales trajectory soars to unprecedented heights. You are playing in a completely different arena that maximizes the value you give and receive.

Chapter 14
Transformational Takeaways

- Sales are about transferring belief. The first people you must transfer that belief to are your advisors.
- Solid sales processes set advisors and clients up for success.
- Congruent sales and marketing efforts give your team and clients confidence.
- Your advisors don't need to know how to do everything like you, but they do need to have a PhD in your process.

Looking to set your sales mindset for scale? Check out additional resources here.

SECTION 7

CULTURE

Have you noticed that in *The Advisor Transformation* I've never once referred to the people who work for me or my advisors as employees? There's a reason for that.

There is no "I" in scale. Scale is a team sport. So no matter how hard you work personally, and how much time you put in, if you don't have a great team that works well together, scale will never happen. Because this is a team sport, everyone on the team must feel they are a valuable member of the team. This feeling is created in every interaction you have with them, from the way you treat them to the words used to describe your relationship with them.

As hard as it may be for some people to believe, you can't scale by brute force. Understand that your success is more dependent on your team than it is on you. So it's critical that you get the most out of your team and that your team pours all their hearts into growing the business, just like you.

#DBDL

Understand that your success is more dependent on your team than it is on you.

This all comes down to culture.

Teammates who are part of a strong culture work harder, are happier, and are more likely to stay. They will care more for the clients and each other, feel less frustration and stress, help you hire other great teammates, and build your business where you see it going. That is why culture is the final piece in Triad's 5 Principles to Scale™.

The first step in creating a great culture is creating an awesome vision for your team, one they can fully buy into and get behind. It's a vision that gets them excited to come to work each day and naturally causes them to fiercely protect the culture. In this section, we'll focus on what creates a great culture and then talk through a few strategies to help you create and protect yours.

You will learn:

- How and why you must constantly and consistently share your vision with the team
- The primary concepts of servant leadership
- Why and how to protect your culture at all costs
- How to hire well
- The two criteria to consider when hiring
- How to create a winning onboarding strategy
- How the team is more critical to culture than you

Are you ready for your next step toward unlimited growth, freedom, and joy?

15

THE ESSENCE OF CULTURE

If the culture is right, success is inevitable. If the culture is wrong, you can kiss the dream goodbye.

Chapter 15 Transformational Targets

- Commit to deescalating internal drama immediately.
- Learn to protect your culture at all costs.
- Practice servant-based leadership.

Throughout *The Advisor Transformation*, we have explored various elements that are crucial for scaling your business, including vision, marketing, sales, and operations. Each of these elements hinges on people buying into them and then executing on the strategies behind them.

Creating a work environment that's conducive to optimal performance is essential because if your teammates believe in the vision, care for the company, and enjoy their surroundings, they will undoubtedly perform better. There is a stark difference between a job where people just clock in and out and a career where individuals believe in the future they are helping to shape.

This distinction underpins the significance of nurturing culture while scaling.

Company culture is a term frequently thrown around, but what does it actually mean?

As defined by the renowned startup and tech publication *Built In*, "Company culture can be succinctly described as an organization's shared ethos. It encompasses the feelings people have about their work, the values they hold dear, their perception of the company's direction, and their contributions to reaching that destination. Together, these attributes characterize the organization's personality or culture." [14]

Recognizing our emotional nature as human beings is also fundamental.

We are flawed, occasionally dysfunctional beings who experience a spectrum of emotions daily. A bad day in a toxic cultural environment can spell catastrophe. However, a challenging

14 https://builtin.com/company-culture

day in a supportive cultural environment can uplift and encourage resilience. The necessity for a positive culture is evident, yet its creation is the most challenging part.

Every leader aspires to cultivate a positive culture, but surprisingly, few of them dedicate time to define what that entails. What kind of culture do we want to establish? What does our team want to be part of? Even those who contemplate these questions rarely devise a plan to instill those beliefs in the team or clarify the what, the why, and the who of culture. Consequently, culture is often left to chance. However, extraordinary cultures are never accidental; they are meticulously manufactured by the leader with intention.

Every leader aspires to cultivate a positive culture, but surprisingly, few of them dedicate time to define what that entails.

Remember Tom from Chapter 6? What a remarkable transformation his story represents.

Tom's ascent in the industry was nothing short of amazing. From bringing on more than $50 million annually and juggling twenty-four appointments in a week, he transformed, increasing his production by more than 70 percent. More impressively, he managed this by trimming down his personal appointments to a mere four per week. Such a feat was not just an achievement but a testament to his shift toward the path of significance.

Tom, as one might expect, was never short of ambition. He exuded a competitive spirit and had an unquenchable thirst to achieve monumental heights. The word courage was practically his middle name, especially when it came to making big moves toward growth. Yet, despite his strengths, a chink in his armor was evident within his team dynamics as he rode the Red Line of Success. Tom's insatiable drive to achieve perfection made him something of a micromanager. He clung to his business like a mother to a newborn baby. Fearful of things not being done correctly, he was a bit of a control freak who couldn't loosen his grip on the day to day.

Then as Tom moved toward the Green Line of Significance™, he had an epiphany. He realized that the more he tried to control his business, the more his business actually controlled him. He realized that the backbone of any successful endeavor was a robust and empowered team who wanted to build alongside him.

Tom realized that culture could no longer be a side project or a wish, but instead it had to be a clear focus to manufacture with intention. He embraced the mission of sculpting an environment where his team would not only thrive but would also love to be part of it.

From the moment Tom stepped into his office, his renewed dedication to the team and culture was obvious. He loved his team and cared for them, but he wanted to show that to them more than ever before. He formed a morning habit of greeting his staff personally, letting them know how much he cared for them. This was a small thing that went over well with Tom's team and reminded him daily that he had an incredible team that chose to be a part of his mission. He implemented bonus structures that benefitted the entire team and aligned with his teams' goals. That ensured that in the end, the entire team would celebrate the growth of the company. He took pride in paying his team members, well above market rate and had the best benefits in town. "If you work for me, you will be spoiled," was his mentality.

His investment in the team extended beyond monetary perks. He dedicated time and resources to team-building retreats and training sessions, even flying seventeen of his staff members to one of Triad's team intensives. He made sure the team worked "on" the business together, rather than just "in" the business.

Many might question the feasibility of such an approach. The reservations would typically revolve around time, cost, and effort. But the repercussions of Tom's focus on culture debunked all such skepticism. While most businesses grapple with the challenge of recruiting top talent, Tom's company became a magnet for potential team members. His reputation for valuing staff meant that he was inundated with resumes. He actually has a whole file of great people who want to work for him. More often than not, these are referrals from existing team members, sparing him the hassle of sifting through numerous cold applications or engaging recruitment agencies.

Furthermore, Tom's investment in fostering a stellar culture has nearly eradicated the company's staff turnover. Every ounce of effort he puts into training a new member is maximized because they stick around. Think about the time, money, and resources wasted to bring a team member in and get them up to speed, just to have them leave and then start the process all over again. When people join Tom's company, they do not leave.

Tom's story underscores a quintessential truth. To manifest a vision of such magnitude, a stellar team is nonnegotiable. And to attract the best in the business, the company needs to be the best for them. Average companies get average people, and those companies don't do exceptional things.

Once the leader has been intentional to manufacture a culture for the best, that is really the start of the process—not the end. Each and every team member has to buy into and understand how critical a role they play in culture.

That is why during team coaching and training sessions, I often pose this straightforward question: "How many of you want to be a part of a great culture, where each and every person cares for each other and creates a an environment where they enjoy coming to work?" Not unsurprisingly, everyone wants this. I then probe further. "It seems we all share this desire. Now comes the challenging part. Whose responsibility is it to create that environment?"

Sometimes those in the training session exchange glances; other times, they realize it's a collective effort. A critical insight about culture is that no person can create it on their own. Leaders and founders must understand that it's not solely their responsibility. Culture is shaped daily by the team's interactions, mindset, and attitude. How do team members treat each other when I am away? Regardless of our differences, all team members share a common goal—to create a positive work environment. When the team acknowledges their collective influence over the company's culture, it's incredibly empowering. How do we respond when someone is having a rough day? Do we gossip behind their back or offer encouragement and support? What are the non-negotiable values that we all adhere to daily?

> Culture is shaped daily by the team's interactions, mindset, and attitude.

As the company expands, maintaining a cohesive culture becomes increasingly challenging. With more people contributing to the culture, differences in values, lifestyles, and political views may arise. These differences can either hinder teamwork or be leveraged as strengths. In Triad's culture, we view differences as assets. The diverse experiences and perspectives enrich our collective wisdom, making us stronger. Despite our differences, we all share a common goal—to create a positive culture for one another. This shared objective is the pillar we cling to rather than the differences that could divide us. We embrace our differences as strengths and focus on the shared mission rather than the differences.

Adopting this perspective is transformative, but it doesn't come naturally; it is a learned behavior. Often, conflicts arise from unspoken expectations. When was the last time we trained our team on being a good culture fit or handling difficult situations?

I learned a valuable lesson during Triad's initial year. A team member who was clearly having a bad day was somewhat curt with a colleague. The colleague, feeling slighted, rallied a group of allies, resulting in three people gossiping and speaking ill of the individual who was merely having an off day. Is it fair to be ostracized by a clique because of a momentary lapse in composure? We addressed the issue by speaking to each team member individually, emphasizing the importance of addressing grievances directly and constructively rather than fostering divisiveness.

This incident underscored the need for training on handling such situations—our responsibility as leaders.

My brother-in-law, a police officer in Oklahoma City, shared a poignant lesson when I was on a ride-along with him in a high-crime area. He explained that approaching potentially dangerous individuals aggressively often escalates the situation. Instead, he adopts a "de-escalate at all times" approach, remaining calm and careful to avoid triggering a confrontation. Imagine if teams adopted a de-escalate drama mindset, addressing conflicts constructively rather than exacerbating them. This approach would significantly minimize the adverse impact on the culture.

Another guiding principle is to assume good intentions during disagreements. Since we share a common mission and goal, it is more constructive to assume positive intentions than malice. Granting grace and assuming the best in each situation fosters a more harmonious culture.

Culture is deeply embedded within an organization. It underpins the organization's vision, teammates, founder, and business trajectory, and all that influences the client experience. For a culture to thrive and consequently for the business to prosper, everyone must understand, own, and safeguard the culture.

We've all seen business owners who make things look easy and others who never seem to get a break. Time and time again, the offices we work with that can't seem to get a break have a culture problem. The owners either never stop to create a culture, or they have a great one that they fail to maintain over time. As a result, they lose teammates, business doesn't go as well as expected, and they come to Triad wondering what happened.

> When aligned with strategy and leadership, a strong culture drives positive organizational outcomes.

When people don't enjoy the culture they work in, they don't put forth their best effort. They stop presenting innovative ideas and—ultimately—leave. If they stay, they may poison the culture you do have. The impact of these actions is hugely disruptive to every organization and can be disruptive well beyond when the person left. Creating a work environment like this makes it impossible to scale.

We all know it takes a whole team to run a business. When you're all moving in the same direction, life is great, but when you're fighting each other, nothing works. That's why having a poor culture is like running uphill with the wind in your face. With the wrong culture, no matter how hard you work, it's nearly impossible to progress. The wind is always in your face. Having a great culture is like running downhill with a tailwind at your back—it allows you to grow faster with less effort.

Let's say you lose one marketer and one advisor in a month. That either slows down or stops your marketing flow, depending on the size of your office, and bottlenecks the sales cycle. Even if you hire a new marketer and a new advisor within a month, you still must train them, get them up to speed on your processes, and then gradually hand them the responsibilities that are sitting there waiting for them. That can take

SCALE

months! Never underestimate the impact of losing good people.

But you can't wave a magic wand and create a great culture. Great culture requires an outstanding vision, intention, and hiring and onboarding practices that will attract the right people with the right mindset to your organization. In this chapter, we'll examine five foundations to creating a great culture.

1. Share your vision
2. Explain the changes
3. Protect the culture at all costs
4. Practice cultural leadership
5. Create cultural alignment

1. Share Your Vision

One of the reasons you must have a vision is that it helps everyone on your team know where you're headed and why. It communicates why you're a great company, which is critical to attracting the all-star teammates you want to hire. This type of person wants to work for something great. They want to rally behind a cause. They don't just want a job. A job is something they can get anywhere. They want to work with a kickass team that is working toward one appealing just cause.

Your just cause is the thing that everyone is working toward.

Years ago, I went to a Mastermind event, and one of the speakers was a guy from Silicon Valley who had completely disrupted the tech sector. I was really excited to hear his take on culture. When he got on the stage, the entire audience was shocked by his age. He was only about twenty-seven, which meant he'd probably started his business when he was twenty-one. But he had created something truly great, so I leaned forward in my seat and prepared for him to lay down some complicated strategies about culture. I figured that if I followed them, I would create the best company culture in the world. But he didn't talk about strategies. Do you know what he said instead?

He said, "In my experience, great people want to work for an exciting company. If your company is doing big things, if you give people something that they're excited to wake up to, and if they feel they're making a difference, your company is unique, and that will do it."

I was shocked.

But he was right.

As he grew his business, leaders from giant corporations voluntarily took pay cuts and joined his relatively unknown startup. This happened in this guy's company, and it has happened at Triad Partners. Several of our teammates have left larger, more established organizations and taken a pay cut to come and work for us. They did it because they can get a paycheck anywhere. What they wanted was a challenge, a just cause, and something they are excited to wake up for.

Everyone at Triad Partners believes in our vision. They understand that we want them and our advisors to live a life of significance. They know that we expect every one of them to Do Business Do Life—**#DBDL**. They know that they're expected to be the best because they work among the best.

Our vision is shared and talked about constantly because it's part of everything we do. Therefore, there's no mistaking what it is. The visibility and clarity of our mission combined with the people we hire allow the culture we want to have flourish. Once you have a great vision, you must understand your role as a leader.

As a leader, you're the one who drives the vision, but your teammates define it. Who you hire, how they show up at work, and how they interact with each other and your clients are what will create a long, sustaining culture.

In a great culture, new hires conform to the culture. In a bad one, the culture conforms to the new hire. That means if you don't have a strong culture and you hire a bully or someone who gossips, your culture will start to tolerate those behaviors. That would never happen in a strong culture. First, it's unlikely that either of those people would get hired. Second, your culture (i.e., your teammates) won't tolerate those behaviors. Either the new hires will change, or they'll be forced to leave.

In teams of fifty people or fewer, every person on that team is a founder of culture. Never forget that.

2. Explain the Changes

A good vision will and should change over time. These changes can affect culture if you fail to let your team know what's happening and why.

As the leader of the vision and the driver behind it, you need to let everyone know why and how the vision is changing when it changes. That keeps teammates on board with the new vision and prevents them from feeling uncertain, which can negatively affect culture. Changing without explaining why is not only confusing but also makes teammates feel left out of the process. It is harder to buy into changes you've been excluded from, and this lack of communication can create friction among teammates.

For example, say you decide to hire an additional receptionist. The way things are running, the receptionist you do have is doing too much. As a result, she's often not at her desk to greet clients. That isn't her fault—her role has expanded to a point where she can't constantly be at the desk. She's doing exactly what you asked her to do. However, if you hire another receptionist without explaining why you need the new hire, your existing receptionist may assume that things had to change because she wasn't good enough at her job. The exact opposite was true. She's so good at her job that you've expanded her responsibilities, and now you need someone else. Your team must understand the changes you make. They must also understand that change is critical in order to grow a successful company, and therefore they must be ready to embrace it when it happens.

3. Protect the Culture at All Costs

When we first started Triad Partners, we gathered a group of team members in a room and turned on a clip of a boxing match between Floyd Mayweather and Victor Ortiz.

If you recall, in this fight, there was very little action until the fourth round when Ortiz broke through Mayweather's defenses with a very light touch. When Mayweather continued to thwart Ortiz's advances with fantastic defense, Ortiz blatantly butted Mayweather, infuriating Mayweather and getting an uproarious response from the crowd.

The ref called a timeout. During the timeout, Ortiz apologized and wanted to hug Mayweather, even wanting to touch Mayweather's gloves. When the fight started back up, Ortiz's gloves were still down. Mayweather smacked Ortiz twice in the head, putting an end to the fight. Mayweather won.

I asked the team about their perspective on the fight. They said Mayweather's move was dirty—he hit Ortiz while his gloves were down. But in boxing, one of the number-one rules is "when you are in the ring, protect yourself at all times." Ortiz dropped his hands, got too comfortable, and got knocked out because he ignored that rule.

This story illustrates a good lesson about culture. Your team must know the number-one rule of the office and protect that at all costs. Triad's number-one rule is to create a great working environment where everybody is excited to work. No matter what happens in a day, we stand by that rule just like Mayweather stood by boxing's top rule regardless of what was going on with Ortiz. Regardless of the emotions or what we feel, we have to protect the culture at all times.

#DBDL

When everyone knows the number-one rule, there's no uncertainty. It means that regardless of what's happening in the day, what the mood is like, or what's going on, everyone knows that protecting the culture is the priority. This is how you protect your culture.

Get clarity on your cultural values and guidelines, and share them with your team over and over again. If you are clear on what those are, more often than not, your team will live up to them.

4. Practice Servant-Based Leadership

Here's something I didn't know early in my career. Leadership is a learned behavior.

The greatest leaders I know practice servant-based leadership, which always puts teammates first. They flip the script of what business owners usually think. So instead of thinking, "What can they do for me?" the question is, "What can I do to help them succeed?" Remember, you are only as strong as your team. When you focus on bringing them up instead of for your own personal gain, you—and they—will be rewarded. They will perform better, align more closely with your mission, and feel that it's their job to help protect company culture. So it's not what your team can do for you but instead what you can do to help them succeed.

Servant leadership focuses on five primary principles: empowerment, growth and development, engagement, collaboration, and ethical behavior.

1. **Empower**: Servant leaders empower their team members by providing them with the necessary tools, resources, and support to excel in their roles. They foster an environment of trust, respect, and collaboration, allowing teammates to contribute their best efforts and ideas.
2. **Provide growth and development opportunities:** Servant leaders are committed to the personal and professional growth of their teammates. They invest in their development through mentorship, coaching, and training opportunities. This focus on growth creates a culture of continuous learning and improvement within the organization. It also gives teammates the chance to become better businesspeople. The better businesspeople they become, the better business you will have. If you agree with this, start by not keeping the lessons in this book a secret—share them with your team.
3. **Foster engagement and satisfaction**: By prioritizing the needs of their teammates, servant leaders create an environment where individuals feel valued and appreciated. That leads to a higher level of teammate engagement and satisfaction since team members are more likely to be motivated, committed, and passionate about their work.
4. **Encourage collaboration and teamwork**: Servant leaders foster a collaborative and team-oriented culture by encouraging open communication, active listening, and shared decision-making. They create a safe space for teammates to express their opinions, ideas, and concerns, which promotes effective teamwork and problem-solving.

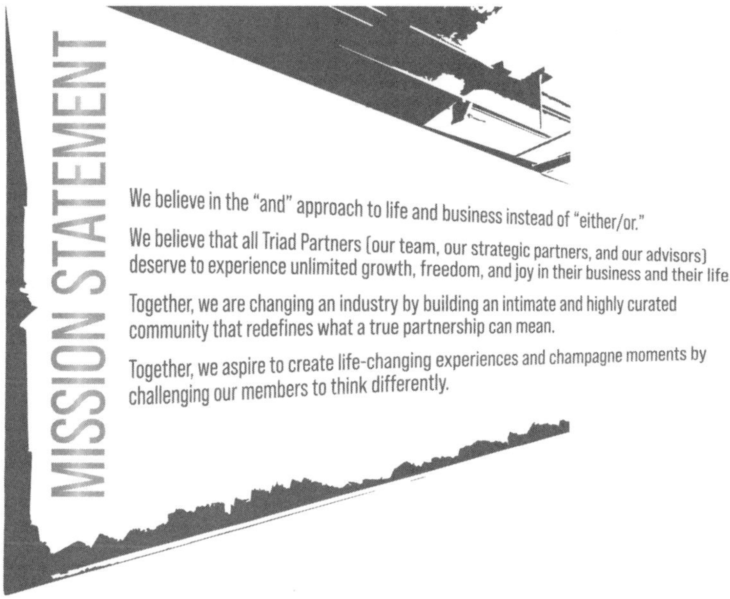

5. **Divisive behavior always kills culture.** You can't have teammates talk about their salaries or gossip about each other if you want to maintain your culture. A house divided will not stand.
6. **Demand ethical and responsible behavior**: Servant leaders demonstrate ethical behavior, integrity, and a commitment to social responsibility. They set a positive example for their teammates and promote a culture of honesty, transparency, and accountability throughout the organization.

On the personal side, servant leaders make sure to protect teammates' personal time. This doesn't just mean ensuring that teammates "turn off" after working hours. It also means noticing and listening to them when they have a rough day. We don't want our teammates to take home the hard stuff. So if they're having a rough day, if mistakes have been made, if workloads have piled up, we make sure managers talk to them and support them so by the time they go home, they feel better. Part of **#DBDL** is also making sure our teammates don't bring business home physically, mentally, or emotionally. When they get home, we want them to enjoy home time. They can return to work the next day.

Chapter 15 Transformational Takeaways

- Good cultures have a de-escalate drama mindset and address conflict head on.
- Having a clear vision and communicating it with teammates not only attracts A-plus players but also gets people excited to work for you.
- Culture has to be protected at all costs by everyone on the team.
- The five traits of servant-based leaders will help elevate your team.
- Cultural alignment gets teammates excited about what they're doing.

16

CREATE A CULTURE THAT SCALES

We used to have such a great culture. But then it was like suddenly, for no reason at all, they all hated working here and wanted to quit.

— Top advisor

Chapter 16 Transformational Targets

- Understand that every single person you hire will define your culture.
- Work on matching cultural fit and aptitude to The Radical Team Development Track™.
- Stop hiring from behind.

An advisor I knew, Luke, had a very successful financial advisory business that included more than 100 teammates and an eight-figure revenue. He had a vision, understood marketing and sales, and had his operations running so well that the business had become a well-oiled machine.

Over the years, one of the biggest compliments Luke and his company received was about their culture.

The teammates loved being part of the company. It was growing quickly, their ideas were heard, and they were in positions that allowed them to grow while also excelling in their areas of expertise. Open communication was a priority, everyone supported each other and the growth of the company, and the team enjoyed going to work. As a result, the number-one way Luke and his team received new team members was through referrals.

However, as Luke and his team experienced more success, the culture started to slip. For starters, Luke started getting a little proud. When he talked about the company's accomplishments, he referred to them as "his." Any mention of his teammates and the roles they had played in creating and running the business fell by the wayside. It wasn't a great feeling for those who had devoted their careers to Luke's vision. Not only did that feel bad, it made them harbor resentment for the work they had done. Some of them started becoming less engaged in their jobs and not as positive about the company, the team, and the mission.

Luke also had become less passionate about the business, which is something that happens when an advisor is on the Red Line. Luke was tired. He felt like he was doing everything because he hadn't scaled the business, and he was often tense and shortsighted.

Luke started spending a lot less time in the office. He hardly ever went in, and when he did, it was to grab something and quickly leave. Normally, that is what we want. Scaling should allow the business owner to start playing the role of the business owner rather than playing the role of the advisor. Seeing them less and less in the office should be an awesome feeling. But that wasn't the case for Luke's team.

For the founder to intentionally be out of the office and have everyone feel good about it, roles and responsibilities have to be passed on to other responsible members of the team. The team also has to be empowered to make decisions, and they have to know that the direction they're moving is producing results.

#DBDL

That wasn't the case for Luke and his team.

"We used to have such a great culture," Luke told me. "But then it was like suddenly, for no reason at all, my entire team hated working here and wanted to quit."

Before Luke reduced his time in the office, he didn't transition from advisor to business owner very well. So when he disappeared, it felt like he became a ghost. When you scale and do it well, disappearing from the office should make teammates feel like they've been entrusted to fully run the show and progress the business.

Even though Luke was gone much of the time and didn't want to be involved in the day-to-day business, he was still viewed as the leader. He hadn't passed the leadership baton or given up control of the day-to-day decisions. So when the team had a pressing decision to make, they contacted Luke, and he responded when he got around to it. This was disheartening for the team since they were still trying to grow.

In addition, because Luke had become more arrogant, he only liked his own ideas and shot down those that came from his team. Often because he was no longer in the mix, he didn't fully understand the context of the idea or why it was suggested. So his ideas, which were the ideas he always chose, came across as "I'm the boss; do it my way." On one occasion, Luke's team discussed an issue and how to resolve it during five consecutive meetings—a couple of week's worth of time. When they ran it by Luke, he shot it down instantly. So much wasted time!

Since Luke wasn't around much, he also lost his personal relationship with and care for the team. He felt that his team members were replaceable, stopped recognizing their efforts, and made it clear that he didn't trust them to grow the business.

As a result, the culture of the company completely changed in a very short period. Many of Luke's best teammates left, and the success of the company started declining. That is what happens when you don't protect your culture. Teammates leave, business declines, and you find yourself right back on the Red Line where you started.

To create the right culture, you must hire the right team. Let's take a look at some hiring and onboarding best practices.

How to Hire Well

When we started Triad, we knew we only wanted to hire A+ people. But as we started hiring, we realized that we had never defined what it means to be an A+ hire.

Is it solely performance-based?

How much does culture play into that?

If someone performs well but doesn't fit the culture, is that okay? We decided that no, it isn't.

For us, an A+ hire is equal parts culture fit and skill/performance. Hiring someone whose performance is off the charts but who negatively affects culture never works. Neither is hiring someone everyone loves and is a great culture fit but can't do their job.

There are two core criteria to consider when deciding whether your new hire, team, or teammates are the right fit.

1. Aptitude (how well they do their job)
2. Culture fit (how well they fit with your culture)

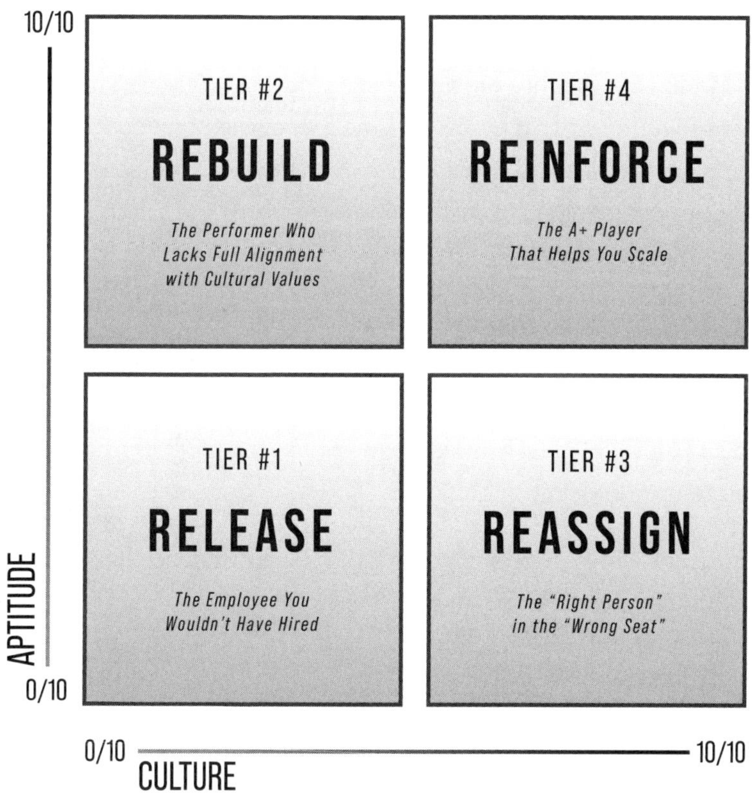

#DBDL

We use something called The Radical Team Development Track™ to identify our A+ players. Once we have identified our A+ players, we use The Radical Team Development Track™ to continue helping them grow and develop. This exercise reveals opportunities of focus, places where we can help them improve as they move through their career at Triad.

In this scoring system, the teammates or possible hire can earn up to ten points each for aptitude and culture fit. Ten is the highest score.

As you can imagine, most people fall somewhere between a ten on culture and a ten on aptitude. Some score combinations can be worked with; others say to us, "This person isn't the right fit." Here are a few examples of how we use The Radical Team Development Track™.

If someone is a five on culture and a five on skills, we consider them transitional. That means it's time to transition them out of the company. The idea is that we can help them transition into something that causes them less stress and is better for them and the company.

From Triad's perspective, we recognize that great companies are not built by hiring people at the transition level. These people aren't excited about what they're doing, and they're not overly skilled at it either. These are not the kind of people we want to hire. Or if we've already hired them, they're the kind of people we will transition (let go).

Let's say that someone scores a ten on performance but is low in the culture area. They are crushing the leader board, but they're running over their teammates. That used to be me, and I had no idea I was doing it until someone pointed it out.

With this type of person, you want to rebuild. This person is really valuable at what they do, but they need to start focusing more on how they impact the team. They can't crush their team. That crushes culture.

Yes, it's important to have high performers, but think about how much better each of them is with a team.

Michael Jordan is a perfect example of how a ten on performance is better with a team. He's the best basketball player of all time. But by himself, could he beat a high school basketball team? No. Even the greatest need their team. If your squad performs better, everyone performs better. So if you have someone who is all performance, you've got to teach them about culture.

So what happens on the other end of the spectrum? Let's say someone is a great culture fit. Everyone loves this person. They do everything they can to bring up everyone around them. Culturally, they are a ten. But their performance? Nothing is happening. They are a one, maybe a two.

With this person, we'll do anything possible to keep them in the company. Part of **#DBDL** is working with people you want to do life with. If we love you, if we want to grab a beer with you, if we think you're interesting and absolutely see that you exude our vision and positively affect the team, we want to try to keep you on the team at all costs.

When we have someone with a culture fit of a ten who is struggling with their role, we dive into where they're struggling and why. The Freedom Compass can come in handy here. Looking through the person's role, we might notice that they're really working on something they don't enjoy and aren't very good at. That's an unhappy and unproductive place for them to be. An example might be someone who is not super detail-oriented working in project management. In these cases, we will look at other roles that are posted within the company and see if we can shift this person to something that is more fulfilling for them and more productive for us.

Sometimes they may just need more training. Whatever the case, we approach this scenario with the attitude that someone who gets your culture can be trained on aptitude. We will exhaust all options before we transition someone out of Triad. We want to give team members every option possible to improve.

The "perfect" person would score a ten in each category, but no one is perfect. For us, A+ is someone who scores an eight out of ten. Special companies are created from the upper fourth quadrant. Therefore, this is where we want each of our team members to be.

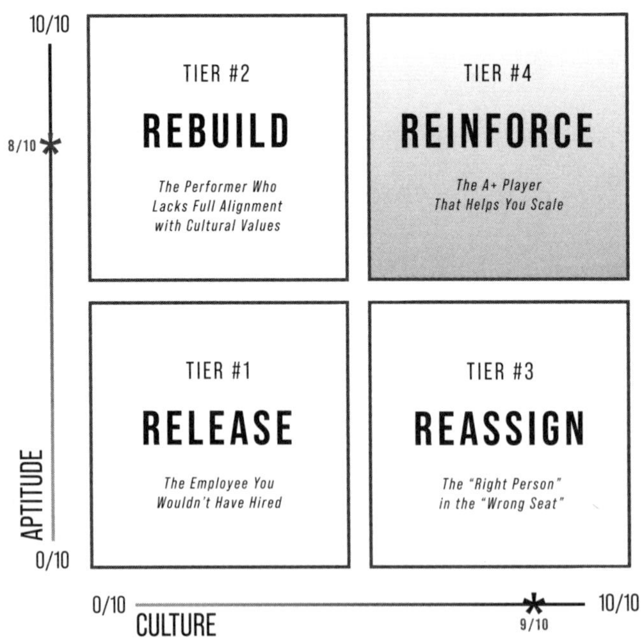

The Top Criteria for Creating an Outstanding Onboarding Process

Onboarding teammates is like taking care of a seed. Do it well, and you'll come back in ninety days and have a beautiful flower. Do it poorly, and when you return you'll wonder what happened. Why isn't it blooming?

Onboarding well is critical to every company's culture. Those who do it well retain teammates, and those who don't do it well lose them.

Your onboarding process should be well-structured and intended to get the new teammates up to speed and out of the storm as quickly as possible. When that new hire graduates from onboarding, they should be more excited about working for you and joining your team than they were when they were hired. If they're excited, ready to do their job, and understand your vision, culture and core values, you know you've done your job. Here's how to create an onboarding process that will set your teammates up for success.

Make sure they're a good fit. The Radical Team Development Track™ is the first part of onboarding because it ensures that to the best of your knowledge, you're hiring people who will succeed in your business and add to your culture.

As part of our onboarding process, we share our core values or set of statements that outline how we work together, how we treat clients, and how our teammates are expected to act. Here are Triad's core values:

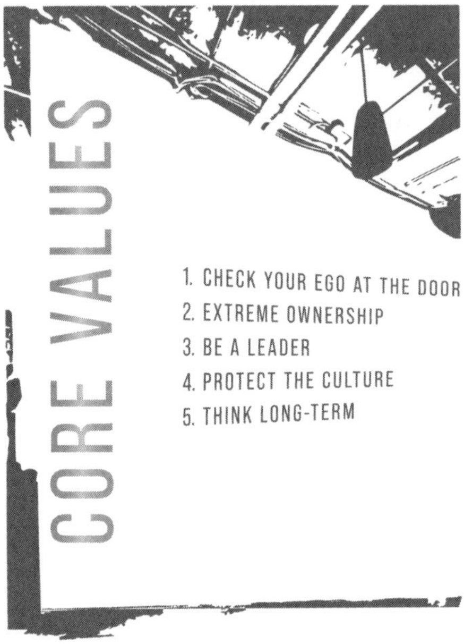

Be clear about what is and isn't going to happen. While your new hire should have a clear understanding of their roles and expectations from the get-go, these need to be fine-tuned during the onboarding process.

For example, if one of your new hire's responsibilities is to bring in new business, what does that mean? How many new clients are they expected to bring in? Is the expectation revenue-based? What is the timeline, and what resources will they have to achieve that goal?

Not only does this set your teammates up for success, it allows them to start running as soon as they're finished with onboarding.

You don't want anyone sitting there saying, "What do I do now?"

At Triad, we also don't give people a fancy title too quickly, and our new hires are aware of this.

Foster a Sense of Belonging and Connectedness. From the minute we start the hiring process, we focus on connection. When we interview someone, we bring a team manager and one other member from that team into the interview process. When possible, we bring the final candidate into the office so they can meet their team.

Once someone is hired, we treat their experience with us in much the same way as we treat our clients. A new hire gets a customized welcome package and is showered with love from our entire community. We actually have a list of seventy-four touchpoints for new hires to ensure that they feel part of our community and don't miss out on anything. These touchpoints include everything from making sure they can access the correct accounts to ensuring that they appear on the organizational chart. They include sending out a survey of their favorite things so we can send them gifts throughout the year.

We use the Enneagram personality test during our hiring process to learn more about the candidate. Once someone is hired, we share their Enneagram number with the rest of our team. This helps all teammates understand how people work and think. Not only does that improve their working relationships, but it also brings them together as a community.

We also create events where our team members build relationships with each other and not just work together. Every year we have Summer Bash, a time when we bring the entire company's families together. No matter where they live, we fly them in with their families, plan events, and spend time together. It's amazing how much care people gain for one another by getting to know each other personally and as friends. They start to understand who they are and where they come from.

Professionally, that helps bridge gaps between parts of the organization, preventing the silo effect. When someone from wealth management and someone from creative end up connecting while playing bags with their kids, that cements a relationship where conversations about the business naturally happen that might not otherwise.

Provide Effective, On-the-Spot Feedback

Does anyone love quarterly or annual reviews? No. They clog up the feedback process and create a lot of unnecessary paperwork that doesn't benefit the organization or the teammates.

At Triad, we give teammates on-the-spot feedback. If quality is lacking, we have a fluid conversation about it. If a deadline was missed, we figure out what happened. Was it unclear? Did the teammates not have the resources they needed to meet it? Was there a miscommunication between management and the teammates?

These conversations are two-way. We expect our teammates to give feedback to their managers about what they could have done better too. It's not just about talking to the teammates. Remember, the better they all are, the better the entire business.

We give feedback on an ongoing basis because we don't like pilling up lists of "things to talk about" and then sitting down and checking them off. Fluid, immediate feedback is better for everyone. It keeps communication open and honest among

Performance Score	**Culture Score**
• Reliability	• Attitude
• Quality of work	• Ethics
• Volume of output	• Impact on others
• Initiative	• Engagement
• Follow through	• Professionalism
• Ownership of role	• Accountability
• Skills and knowledge	• Ego
• Capacity	• Flexibility

teammates, teams, and supervisors, and it allows people to move and improve quickly.

While we don't give feedback publicly, we do it quickly because we believe that honest feedback won't break anyone. If you were doing something you could improve on, wouldn't you want someone to tell you?

The Enneagram numbers come in handy here. They help us understand how to approach each individual in a way that resonates with them and leads to the best end result.

Once a year, we evaluate our teammates using The Radical Team Development Track™ that we talked about earlier. Through this process, managers rank them from one to ten.

Once we know which tier the teammate falls into—one through four on The Radical Team Development Track™—leaders then have the proper information and are empowered to continue the development process with their team.

Avoid Reactive Hiring

The hiring process we just walked through takes time. So what happens if you need someone right this minute? Once again, I challenge you to look at your mindset. When you need someone right now, it says that you're hiring from behind. That often leads to reactive hiring, which will not bring you to scale. It is a common mistake in our industry.

Many advisors operate lean until they realize their team is overwhelmed. Then they hastily hire out of desperation. This burdens an already overtaxed staff with training new hires, fostering a toxic environment for newcomers. This reactive approach—addressing business needs hastily—results in erratic growth and is an Enemy of Scale. To scale smoothly, anticipate future needs in your vision. Imagine training someone for three to six months before they are needed. Then when the business requires them, they thrive rather than struggle.

This approach yields steady growth. Furthermore, if you want to build something to scale, hiring shouldn't be your side project; it should be your main focus. We have reverse engineered advisors' organizational charts as they've grown. If your business doubles over the next months, who will your next two hires need to be? What roles will they have? It's crucial to having foresight in your vision versus guessing wrong.

Another hiring consideration is quality. To be the best, hire the best. Advisors often hire based on cost, resulting in subpar outcomes. It is better to overpay for the right person than to constantly replace unsuitable hires. It is thus crucial to match the right people with the right positions. Hire first who is best for the role. Don't hire thinking,

"I like them; we can make it work." The business should determine who you hire, not your emotional attachment or their likability. This is a common mistake many advisors make, resulting in new hires lacking a clear role or job description and struggling to find their identity. Roles vary in skill and experience requirements. Understanding that will guide your hiring process.

For medium to high-skill roles, avoid hiring inexperienced individuals. That is risky. They may lack necessary skills, take too long to train, or dislike the job. For low-skill roles, entry-level candidates are suitable. For medium- to high-skill roles, seek candidates who already have the required skills. For high-skill roles, target individuals with relevant experience who enjoy and excel in that role. Such hires will enhance the company from day one due to their expertise.

To be the best, hire the best. Advisors often hire based on cost, resulting in subpar outcomes. It is better to overpay for the right person than to constantly replace unsuitable hires.

Another key is having a clear job description with detailed roles and responsibilities. If you don't have it, you shouldn't hire. When this is complete, attract your new team members in the same way you attract new clients. Have a structured process, and actively pursue top prospects.

These teammates will contribute more to your business growth than new clients. Rarely are these individuals actively job hunting. Most of them are content and loyal in their current roles. Implement a process to gauge their openness to conversation, and progressively sell your company's vision. For example, in Triad's three-year-old business, only two hires resulted from traditional Indeed or LinkedIn ads. Passive recruitment doesn't attract the caliber of candidates we seek. Instead, we identify potential candidates and engage them through a sales process, typically beginning with a fifteen-minute call to assess openness and share our vision. This progresses to a one-hour, face-to-face meeting, followed by another meeting. Usually, by the end of this process, candidates are enthused about our vision and culture. And they're eager to join us. Remember, hiring is a process.

Chapter 16

Transformational Takeaways

- Who you hire defines your culture.
- If you hire A+ teammates, define what that means.
- The Radical Team Development Track™ hires on aptitude and culture fit.
- Your onboarding process must make the new teammate feel at home and set them up to successfully do their job.
- Hiring from behind makes scaling impossible.

Looking to set your culture for scale? Check out additional resources here.

THE FINAL STEP

COMMIT TO THE TRANSFORMATION

Congratulations! You've gone through these pages and reached the final chapter. Yet, as one chapter concludes, another begins—the chapter of action. Equipped with the belief, insights, vision, and methodologies to cultivate a business of significance, you will see the real challenge emerge. It's not merely about comprehension but implementation. To truly achieve this transformation, you can't dabble. You must go all in.

Regardless of where you are in your career—just getting started, midway, or in the final chapter—it is never too late to change the trajectory of where you want to go.

Regardless of where you are in your career—just getting started, midway, or in the final chapter—it is never too late to change the trajectory of where you want to go. One of my advisors who is thirty years into his career once reflected with a heavy sigh, "That Red Line almost killed me." He was stuck on the hamster wheel, sacrificed his health, and saw his physical condition deteriorate. But eventually, he took a deep breath, recognized the loop he was in, and transformed his approach. Today, he lives a more balanced life than ever before. His only regret? Not learning it sooner. You don't have to make these sacrifices.

I'm often reminded just how important this next step is. As you've seen, the closest you will ever be to the transformation is today. Each day that goes by, you can lose energy, focus, and excitement for what could be. Over time, the possibility of a genuine transformation can drift away. So don't procrastinate or delay. Jump on the Green Line of Significance™ now.

Life has often nudged me time and time again to be intentional with my life. And I want you to do the same. We only have so much time. Why not pursue a life of significance with the time we have?

About a year into my business, I had a sobering reminder of this.

A good friend and advisor I've worked with over the years called me out of the blue and asked if I could help his friend. He was a younger advisor who had some questions.

Of course, I was happy to have a conversation with him.

As the friend, Kevin, and I started talking, he shared that his life had completely changed over the last couple of years. He felt it crucial to share his journey with me for context.

You see, he had worked under another advisor, Joe, for over a decade. Joe was renowned as one of the top producers in the industry with all the accolades to prove it. Joe was Kevin's mentor, and Kevin was proud to be Joe's "key support person" doing everything to aid Joe in his pursuit. Joe, with his intense work ethic and dedication, relied heavily on Kevin and others for support.

However, a turning point arrived a few years ago. Joe called a team meeting and delivered devastating news. He had been diagnosed with an incurable cancer with limited time left. But this wasn't merely a revelation; it was a call to action for the team.

For Kevin and the team, the day of Joe's transition marked a complete professional metamorphosis. From being supporters, they became the torchbearers, taking the business into their own hands, rallying together, undergoing significant restructuring, and ultimately, achieving a remarkable transformation.

Sadly, Joe passed away eighteen months after that poignant meeting. But Kevin was proud of the team's resilience and ability to carry forth Joe's legacy.

Now, Joe wasn't armed with all the information and insights from this book when he was forced to change the way he did business. Suppose that before his diagnosis, Joe had changed his processes to scale so instead of transitioning out of sheer desperation, his motivation to transition came from the thrill of realizing that his team, his clients, and his family would benefit immensely from a thriving, resilient business.

Reflecting on the journey of that particular team, a question lingered in my mind: "What if Joe had built his business this way right from the start of his career?" How much more fulfilling would his journey have been, both for him and his team, had they initiated this transformation earlier, not just as a response to a dire prognosis?

Yet another advisor I know, immensely successful by most standards, found himself at a crossroads. Business flowed smoothly, but enthusiasm had waned. Despite trying various adjustments, including reducing his hours, a sense of fulfillment remained elusive. Ultimately, he realized he had lost his purpose. He had achieved his definition of success but lacked a clear vision for future growth. Adopting a new perspective transformed his approach. He rekindled his "day-one mentality," and approached each day with renewed vigor, eagerly anticipating growth and the possibilities ahead.

I truly believe you should build your business as if your life depends on it because in many ways, it does. The quality of your life, the freedom, and the joy hinge significantly on the relationship you foster with your business. Sadly, many don't grasp the gravity of this and end up entangled in ventures that don't resonate with their core values.

The journey to a significant business isn't just about sheer effort but entails directed, strategic endeavors. It's a long-term commitment that requires relentless focus and periodic adjustments. Remember, procrastination is progress's worst adversary. As the days go by, it becomes increasingly easy to revert to old habits. But you have the power to chart a new course. Embrace the Green Line of Significance™.

I ask you to commit to the Green Line of Significance™ going forward. That's why I wrote this book.

The path is in your grasp, ready to be fulfilled.

It's time to create the transformation.

TOP DBDL TAKEAWAYS

#DBDL

Are you ready to transformation your business and your life so that you can #DBDL? Here's the top #DBDL highlights from *The Advisor Transformation.*

1. Rather than double your production, grow a business that is half as dependent on you as it is now.

2. Relate your success to how much your stress decreases over time.

3. Leverage human capital to accomplish more in less time.

4. If you have the capital, invest it in teammates so that you can get the team and infrastructure in place that you need to scale.

5. Set clear milestones, determine what you must do to reach them, and measure your progress beyond production.

6. Create an exciting vision that your whole team and your clients can rally around.

7. Release the fear that when you delegate something to a trusted team member, it won't be done correctly.

8. Let your team become "partners" in running the business because this will encourage them to think about future challenges and opportunities.

9. Differentiate yourself by showing clients that you go beyond the basics of retirement planning and instead offer a comprehensive plan.

10. Deliver on all of your promises and pay attention to every interaction that you or your team have with your clients

11. Do not rely on brute force for growth.

12. Understand that leadership is a learned behavior, not something that you're born with.

13. For a leader/founder to leave the office for a period of time and feel good about it, roles and responsibilities must be passed to other responsible members of the team.

14. Find a structure for identifying A+ players and helping them grow and develop.

TOP ENEMIES OF SCALE

As much as you want to look for #DBDL opportunities as you scale, you also want to avoid enemies of scale. Here are some of the top enemies of scaled identified in *The Advisor Transformation.*

1. Resolve to make a change and then never get started.

2. Rally the team in hopes of spreading out the workload and then don't provide direction to them.

3. Hire new team members with the mentality that throwing people at your problems will fix them.

4. Take on a business partner to spread out your workload.

5. Shift your mindset toward scale enthusiastically and then give up.

6. Approach work with the mindset that if something is to be done correctly, it must be done by you.

7. Lack clarity in where you're going and how you plan to get there.

8. Make excuses for not advancing or scaling as quickly or as effectively as you want to.

9. Believe that you are the only one who can help your clients because you are the one who “brought them in”.

10. When you are training people in your sales process, overwhelm them with information.

11. Underestimate the impact of losing good people.

LOVED THE CONTENT IN *THE ADVISOR TRANSFORMATION*, BUT ARE NOT SURE HOW TO GET STARTED?

DON'T BE AFRAID TO ASK MY TEAM FOR HELP!

My team and I work to help advisors get more growth, freedom, and joy from their business and life so let us do what we do best.

LET US HELP!

While *The Advisor Transformation* lays the foundation for creating more growth, freedom, and joy in your business and life, our world class team can give you the extra boost you need to start implementing these principles so that you can scale your business today.

Contact us here
www.theadvisortransformation.com

ABOUT THE AUTHOR

Shawn Sparks has worked with hundreds of advisors throughout his career, showing them how to be better business owners and better wives and mothers, husbands and fathers. His company coined the phrase "Do Business, Do Life" (#DBDL) as a testimony to the possibility of achieving balance as a busy advisor.

As a business development expert, Shawn shows top advisors how to create a comprehensive marketing, sales, and operations plans that allow them to do more in less time. His mission is to show advisors strategies for scaling their business that truly supports the lifestyle they desire–while avoiding burnout and improving all aspects of their lives.

Shawn puts what he teaches into practice. As the owner of a growing business development firm, husband, and father, he knows firsthand what it's like to grow a business while raising a young family. Although he loves his work, his greatest joy is found in spending time with his four kids: Sadie, AnnMarie, Sutton, and Charlotte and his wife, Aubrey.

www.theadvisortransformation.com

ABOUT TRIAD PARTNERS, LLC

Triad is a business development company that helps overwhelmed financial advisors experience unlimited growth, freedom, and joy in their business and their life.

Together with Triad members, Triad is changing an industry by building an intimate and highly curated community that redefines what a true partnership can mean.

Triad believes in the "and" approach to life and business instead of "either/or" (#DBDL) and believes its teams and members deserve to live #DBDL.

www.triadpartners.com

DOWNLOAD THE AUDIOBOOK FREE!

AS A THANK YOU FOR BUYING MY BOOK, I WOULD LIKE TO GIVE YOU THE AUDIOBOOK FOR FREE

Read it in the car, on a walk, or in your spare time and unlock the exciting future that this book can help you create.

Your transformation awaits; get the audiobook for FREE at the link below.

THEADVISORTRANSFORMATION.COM